TESTED *in the* TRENCHES

A 9-STEP PLAN FOR BUILDING AND SUSTAINING A MILLION-DOLLAR FINANCIAL SERVICES PRACTICE

Ron Carson, CFP®, CFS, ChFC, and Steve Sanduski, MBA, CFP®

Dearborn™
Trade Publishing
A **Kaplan Professional** Company

This publication is designed to provide accurate and authoritative information in regard to the subject matter covered. It is sold with the understanding that the publisher is not engaged in rendering legal, accounting, or other professional service. If legal advice or other expert assistance is required, the services of a competent professional person should be sought.

Vice President and Publisher: Cynthia A. Zigmund
Acquisitions Editor: Mary B. Good
Senior Managing Editor: Jack Kiburz
Interior Design: Lucy Jenkins
Cover Design: Scott Rattray, Rattray Design
Typesetting: the dotted i

Published by Dearborn Trade Publishing
A Kaplan Professional Company

Printed in the United States of America

05 06 07   10 9 8 7 6 5 4 3 2 1

Library of Congress Cataloging-in-Publication Data

Carson, Ron.
    Tested in the trenches : a 9-step plan for building and sustaining a million-dollar financial services practice / Ron Carson, Steve Sanduski.
      p.   cm.
    Includes index.
    ISBN 1-4195-0158-5 (7.25x9 hardcover)
    1. Financial planning industry—Vocational guidance. I. Sanduski, Steve. II. Title.
HG179.5.C365 2005
332.6′023′73—dc22

                                            2004025395

To my wife, Jeanie, and our three great kids, Chelsie, Madison, and Grant, who provide meaningful purpose in my life

—Ron Carson

To Linda—you make my compelling vision of the future a reality every day. And to Paige, Cori, and Tenley, the joy you bring into my life is immeasurable.

—Steve Sanduski

Contents

"The journey of a thousand miles begins with a single step."
—CHINESE PROVERB

By picking up this book, you've signaled that you're at a fork in the road.

If your career as a financial advisor was laid out along a time continuum, you'd notice that over time you came to many decision-making forks in the road. Along the way, you had to decide which firm to align yourself with; what marketing plans to implement; what staff to hire; which location to set up your office; whether to get paid by commissions, fees, or both; which products to sell; and what software systems to implement. In this book, we are going to ask you to make one more decision.

Here are your two choices:

1. You can continue to do things the way you've always done them and continue to get the same results.
2. Or, you can choose to take the "road less traveled" and make significant improvements in your business and your life.

By picking up this book, you've signaled that you're ready to pursue choice #2.

Will it be easy? Will it happen quickly? Of course not. But one thing we can promise you, you're going to get there much faster with our help than you would hunting and pecking on your own.

So where is "there," you ask. The sad truth is, very few people know where "there" is for *them*. They are so busy letting life live them instead of living life. They're spending their time putting out the fires of life instead of igniting those fires. And at the end of the day, they realize they sped through and passed by more than they caught up to.

Does any of this resonate with you? Finding your "there" is the initial critical step for making your business and your life happen. Many advisors that we work with want to skip this step. They want to jump right into marketing, right into bringing in the bucks. Well, you know what? Let's suppose for just a moment that you skipped our first step and, through sheer luck or good karma, you built a very profitable business. What you'll likely find is, you won't be any happier with a million-dollar practice than you were with a $250,000 practice. If you disagree, talk to lottery winners.

Money doesn't buy happiness. Ah, but money coupled with meaningful purpose, clarity, and direction is a recipe for unlimited happiness, opportunity, and legacy.

That leads us to the first secret to success in our business, *Relentless Burning Desire*. Relentless Burning Desire is more than just motivation; it's more than just a shot of adrenaline. Relentless Burning Desire is an ongoing passion and enthusiasm for your work and your life. Those who have Relentless Burning Desire know exactly what they want out of life, and they have a game plan to strive toward it. Sure, they still come across many of the same trials and tribulations that we each confront in life, but as German philosopher Friedrich Nietzsche said, "He who has a strong enough why can bear almost any how."

Here's the bad news. We cannot give you Relentless Burning Desire. It comes from within. But what we can do is help you ignite it. We can give you a track to follow that will guide you toward finding your Relentless Burning Desire. Through our Blueprinting exercises, you'll engage in some serious contemplation, answer thought-provoking questions, and, if you're honest with yourself, you'll find and ignite your Relentless Burning Desire.

Once you've found your Relentless Burning Desire, the hardest part is over. Yes, there will still be tough times ahead, but with your newfound purpose, the tough times will be much more manageable and you'll be able to keep things in perspective.

After you've built your foundation by igniting your Relentless Burning Desire, you'll move to the second secret to success, to *deliver world-class service through Love Affair Marketing*.

Think back to a time when you experienced an extraordinary and unexpected level of kindness and service. It may have happened in the most unexpected situation. For Steve, it happened at the local grocery store:

> My wife and I were having a big party, so I went to the store to pick up a few goodies. When I got home I realized I was missing a 12-pack of root beer. So I called the store and explained that somehow between the checkout and my car, the 12-pack had disappeared. The young clerk on the other end of the phone was very understanding and said, "Would it be OK if I stopped by your house and delivered the pop to you?" I said that would be great. Then he asked, "If I delivered it in the next 30 minutes, would that be quick enough?" I said that would be terrific.
>
> About 25 minutes later, there was a knock on my door and the store employee proudly gave me a 12-pack of root beer. Then he looked at me and said, "For all your trouble, here's a gallon of vanilla ice cream so you can make some root beer floats." Wow. I was stunned. I was not accustomed to this level of service, especially from a young clerk at a grocery store.
>
> As a result of this extraordinary and unexpected level of kindness and service, I've become an evangelist for this particular grocery store. Not only do I shop there, I've also shared this story with many of my friends. I'm sure they've received a thousandfold return on that gallon of vanilla ice cream.

Ironically, a couple of days later, I was cleaning out the van and, to my astonishment, discovered the original 12-pack of root beer—it was resting quietly underneath the backseat where it slid during the drive home from the store.

This level of client service is what we call Love Affair Marketing. Love Affair Marketing means doing things that are so extraordinary, so unexpected, and so genuine, that your clients will become your evangelists and will send you referrals from people who are like them. It's all about emotional reciprocity and building a *genuine*, service-based relationship with your clients.

Here's a fact: Financial services is a commodity business. You cannot differentiate yourself by generating better performance, delivering better financial plans, or having access to certain products. Our business is too competitive and filled with too many brilliant people to allow a chosen few to get ahead and stay ahead of the crowd through performance, plans, or products. You may not agree, but that has been our experience and our bias, so you need to be aware of it.

With that said, you cannot be a performance cellar-dweller either and expect to survive long term. As long as you're reasonably close to market returns, deliver professional plans, and have access to a wide variety of products, you'll be on the same playing field as every other advisor.

Now here's some good news. The idea that financial services is a commodity business is extremely liberating. This means you don't have to spend 60 hours a week searching for alpha (let the mutual fund companies do it for you). In a commodity business, you differentiate yourself through service, brand, and relationship.

Differentiating yourself through service, brand, and relationship is the only sustainable competitive advantage available to you. Notice that we said sustainable. We'll always have the guru who puts up a few consecutive years of stellar performance and builds a big business. Remember Henry Kaufman and Joe Granville in the early 1980s? How about Robert Prechter in the mid to late 1980s? And none of us can forget Elaine Garzarelli and her frizzy hair and Hanes commercial. In the late 1990s, we had the rise of Abby Joseph Cohen and the Internet stock managers and analysts.

Guess what all of them had in common? They had their 15 minutes of fame and then flickered out. They were not able to build a sustainable business on their market prowess. The laws of probability tell us that we will always have these types of people. In fact, if we assume we have a 50-50 chance of outperforming the market in any given year, then one out of every 1,024 investment managers theoretically should beat the market for ten years in a row. *Theoretically* is the operative word here. In reality, how many mutual fund managers beat the market (i.e., the S&P 500 Index) for ten consecutive years ending December 2004? The answer: fewer people than the fingers on your left hand.

Don't get us wrong; we're not indicting the investment management industry—quite the contrary. It's a testament to the competitiveness and brilliance of investment managers that they are all (almost all) able to perform within such a tight band of performance when measured over any reasonable period of time, such as five to ten years. Who you choose to work with in this group of investment managers (and other service providers for that matter) boils down to, you guessed it, service, brand, and relationship.

It's easy to say you provide great service, but it's an entirely different matter to deliver it. Take a look at the airlines. We'd be hard-pressed to find a sorrier bunch of service providers. In fact, when asked why he chose to fly Southwest Airlines, management guru Tom Peters said, "If I'm going to get crappy service, I might as well pay as little as possible for it."

Despite the inconvenience, you should be happy when you receive poor service. Why? Because it makes your job as a financial advisor much easier. Every time you receive poor service, tap your wallet or purse, because it's going to get fatter. How? Poor service providers lower your clients' expectations, thus making it easier (and more appreciated) for you to step in and deliver world-class service. Notice we said world-class service. There's a big difference between "good" service and "world-class" service. In fact, the difference could be about $1 million a year.

Good service is the bare minimum necessary to compete in our business. As you'll learn, world-class service is completely different. It's a much more severe standard, and by achieving it, you'll position yourself as the go-to advisor in your market. World-class service will then become part of your brand. Your brand is simply what people think of when they hear your name. As a test, ask the next few clients you meet what they think of when they hear the name of your firm. If there's not an immediate, definitive reaction, you have no brand. You're simply lost in the clutter.

Starbucks coffee.

No doubt you had a reaction when you read those two words. Starbucks has developed a brand that for most people evokes positive feelings, emotions, and thoughts. Starbucks delivers an "experience" that is part of its brand. By developing and delivering an experience for your clients, you'll create an unassailable business that will go a long way toward helping you attract and retain high-quality clients.

Then there are relationships. If all of your clients were lined up in a row, could you walk down the line and greet each of them by his or her first name? Would you feel comfortable hugging them? If you're a typical advisor, the answer is probably no. The reason is that most advisors have "accounts"—not relationships. Getting more accounts will not move you to million-dollar production, but getting more relationships will.

Prior to its breakup, AT&T had a popular advertising slogan. It was simply "Reach Out and Touch Someone." Notice AT&T did not say "Reach Out and Call Someone" or "Reach Out and Communicate with Someone." It specifically used the word *touch,* which for a high-tech company was a brilliant move. AT&T realized that it was not in the telecommunications business. It was in the business of *connecting* people. Unfortunately, in more recent years, AT&T has forgotten what business it was in.

At its core, most technology is about enabling relationships. Cars are not simply a mode of transportation; they enable people who are in different locations to come together. They enable people to share good times by getting them from one location to another location. Airplanes do the same thing. Computers and e-mail allow people to connect with other people all over the world. And the list goes on.

So when you look at the business we're in, remind yourself that it's not about products; it's about people. When you focus on people first, you develop a relationship that transcends business to consumer. You end up connecting with people, understanding their needs at a core level, and then you can develop and deliver solutions that fit and work for them. That's Love Affair Marketing.

The third secret to success is to *Systematize Everything*. Systemization is the mechanism that keeps you focused on your Relentless Burning Desire and allows you to deliver Love Affair Marketing on a consistent basis.

We're going to broaden the definition of a system. For our purposes, a system could be one of the following:

1. A ritual
2. A written procedure
3. A checklist

Staying focused on your Relentless Burning Desire requires rituals. One of the first things you'll learn from us is the importance of developing a vision and a mission and setting goals. But just writing them on paper is not enough. You need to develop a ritual that involves reading each of these documents every single day. Try laminating them and placing them on the mirror behind your bathroom sink.

Implementing your vision, mission, and goals is not easy. In particular, turning your goals into completed goals requires tremendous tenacity to accomplish the activities necessary to get results. And when the road is tough, your vision and mission (if they were done correctly) will give you the impetus to persevere and keep moving forward.

Delivering Love Affair Marketing relies more heavily on procedures and checklists. You'll soon learn that we are extremely meticulous about detail. No detail is too small to escape our attention. And we have to be that way. Why? Because we're in a service and relationship business, and in that kind of business, people focus on the details.

In order to get the details right, we systematize everything. We have a system for the Director of First Impression's morning and afternoon office procedures. We have a system for scheduling client appointments. We have a system for following up with prospects. In all, we have hundreds of systems, and they're all codified in our Systems Manual. Overkill? Not if you want to consistently deliver world-class service.

The worst thing you could do is begin delivering a higher level of service and then, through lack of a system, lower that service level. Once clients become used to a certain level of service, they don't want to go back to the "old way."

There are two ways you can prevent slipping back into the old way. First, you have to have great staff. Second, you have to have great systems. That one-two punch is an unbeatable combination. Keep in mind that poorly written systems—or no systems at all— can cause extraordinary people to generate mediocre results. In our business, we need great systems and great people to get great results.

Relentless Burning Desire, Love Affair Marketing, and Systemization make up the philosophical framework that underpins everything we do. Within this framework, we have nine *Tested in the Trenches* (or TNT) ideas that translate these three concepts into practical, actionable steps you can implement.

What you have in your hands right now is literally worth millions of dollars. But like a Van Gogh painting, you have to do something in order to realize that stored value. In Van Gogh's case, you would have to sell the paining. In your case, you have to *IM-PLEMENT*. We're not big on capitalizing words, but we want to make our point clear:

> Simply reading this book without implementing the ideas is like exercising without sweating—you think you're helping yourself but you're really just wasting your time.

If you have a sincere desire to make significant improvements in your business and your life, then clear your schedule, read this book, and go back and implement each TNT idea in the order it is presented. By doing so, you'll join the rarefied group of personally fulfilled and professionally successful top achievers.

In Robert Frost's wistful poem *The Road Not Taken*, a traveler comes to a fork in the road and decides to take the one less traveled. At the end of the poem, the traveler reflects and realizes that taking the road less traveled made all the difference. Our hope is that by reading this book and implementing these ideas, you'll look at *your* fork in the road and confidently decide to take the one less traveled. And 10, 20, or 30 years from now, when you're reflecting on your life's accomplishments, you too will say it has made all the difference.

GAIN PERSONAL AND PROFESSIONAL CLARITY THROUGH THE BLUEPRINTING PROCESS

1

BUILD THE FOUNDATION

"The unexamined life is not worth living."
—SOCRATES

In 1988, a devastating wildfire destroyed nearly 800,000 acres in Yellowstone National Park. The charred remains looked about as full of life as the dark side of the moon. Yet within a very short period of time, those blackened remains were teeming with more than 2,000 germinated tree seedlings per acre. And no, they weren't planted by the Boy Scouts. Instead, Mother Nature did her magic.

Yellowstone is blanketed with a tree called the lodgepole pine. The lodgepole pine is a unique tree because it has two ways of replicating itself. First, it can replicate like other trees by dropping seeds onto the forest floor. Unfortunately, the forest is frequently so thick that there's not enough sunlight reaching the floor for the seeds to take root. So the resourceful lodgepole pine trees have developed a second way to replicate. Instead of dropping all their seeds at once, they wisely hold back some of their seeds in cones that are glued shut with a resin. The lodgepole pine then waits for an opportune time to release the seeds when the odds of germination are the greatest. Here's where it gets interesting.

In the forest, careless campers or lightning eventually start a fire that clears out the underbrush and opens the way for sunlight. But the fire does something else equally important. It heats up the resin on the cones, which allows the cones to open and drop their remaining seeds. These newly dropped seeds take root in the nutrient-rich ash and absorb the sunlight that now reaches the forest floor. Before long, a new forest is sprouting from the ashes.

Being a financial advisor today feels a lot like being a lodgepole pine. Business was good for many years and our practices grew as prosperous as a thick forest. But then came our intense fire in the form of a nasty bear market in the early 2000s.

Now that the bear market fire has cooled, how you will respond is the question that remains. We believe that locked up inside of yourself are the seeds of new life. But like the lodgepole pine, you may need an outside force to heat you up. As coaches, we can help you start the fire, but it's up to you to take advantage of the heat and develop your own Relentless Burning Desire.

Completing the Blueprinting exercises is the key to igniting your Relentless Burning Desire. Igniting your Relentless Burning Desire requires you to dig deep. You have to spend some serious time reflecting, contemplating, and being authentic with yourself. This is not something you're going to knock out in a weekend. It could take weeks or even months before it fully evolves into a clear picture of your future.

So what is Blueprinting? Blueprinting is a series of five exercises that will help you develop a crystal clear map of where you want to go personally and what you want to accomplish professionally. This new clarity will help make your life much more meaningful and your business much more profitable.

You may have already been through this type of process, but perhaps it's been a while. That's fine, because revisiting the process will help you determine if some tweaking is in order. If this is

T*he Five Blueprinting Exercises*

1. Identifying your values—certain things are important to you, but are you living those values day in, day out?
2. Finding your meaningful purpose in life—what are you "called" to do that will be remembered long after you're gone?
3. Creating a compelling vision for your future—how can you achieve success and significance if you don't know what they look like?
4. Developing a personal and professional mission statement—once you know where you're trying to go, wouldn't it be easier to get there with a map?
5. Setting SMAC-certified goals (specific, measurable, achievable, compatible)—wouldn't it be helpful to track your progress along the way?

your first attempt at achieving clarity about your future, then congratulations. You're about to embark on a process that will literally change your life.

WHAT CAN BLUEPRINTING DO FOR YOU?

Blueprinting can do several things for you. First of all, you'll take the time to step back, reflect, and reevaluate. You'll discover what's going right and what's going wrong—both personally and professionally. You'll figure out what changes you would like to make and then create a plan to overcome what's presently stopping you from making those changes. It's easy to get so busy doing "stuff" as we go through life that we really lose sight of the big picture. Blueprinting helps you become focused again on the big picture.

Second, Blueprinting helps you zero in on the things that are most important to you and that are critical in your life. Equally important, it gives you a mechanism to help you spend more time doing those things. If you've ever been to a horse race, you may have noticed that some of the horses wear blinders. Blinders limit the horses' peripheral vision, so they stay focused on the path ahead of them. By identifying what's important in your life and then putting on blinders, you can stay focused on the road ahead and not let the noise of business or life get in the way.

Third, Blueprinting helps you find meaningful purpose in your life. You'll understand the impact you're supposed to make in this world. You'll figure out how you can contribute to the betterment of your family, your friends, your community, and your church. You'll identify the "why" behind what you are doing and the meaning behind what you are doing. Knowing your purpose allows you to get out of bed in the morning and feel great about the kind of person you are and the type of life you are leading.

Fourth, Blueprinting helps you find direction. Are you heading the right way? Do you even know where you are heading? You'll look inward at your internal compass and determine where it wants to lead you. Yogi Berra once said, "When you get to the fork in the road, take it." The key is to not just stand there and do nothing. By following your path, you'll be pleasantly surprised where it leads you.

And, fifth, Blueprinting helps you find fulfillment. You see, if you do all these things—take the time to reevaluate your life, focus on those things that are most important to you, identify your purpose, and find your sense of direction—fulfillment will ensue as naturally as the caterpillar turns into a butterfly. You'll get the feeling that everything's going great, and you'll jump out of bed full of energy and enthusiasm for life even before the alarm clock blares.

BLUEPRINTING HELPS YOU CONNECT WITH CLIENTS

You may be wondering what all this has to do with getting new clients. The answer: everything. Imagine this scenario. It's your first meeting with a prospect. He's been ushered into your office, you've exchanged pleasantries and gotten to know each other a little bit, and now it's time to get down to business.

Prospect: *So, John, I'm here because Mike Smith suggested I meet with you. He knew I was unhappy with my current advisor, and he felt you could help me. What I'd like to know is what makes you different from my present advisor?*

Advisor: *Well, Paul, that's a great question. I believe we provide the best service, offer great advice, and really take care of our clients. We've been in business for 18 years, through bull and bear markets, and we wouldn't have survived if we didn't do a good job for our clients.*

Prospect: *My last advisor said pretty much the same thing. Can you be more specific about what you do that makes you different?*

Advisor: *Sure. We offer our clients quarterly consolidated statements so you can see how all of your assets are doing, regardless of where they are held. We also handle all inquiries to our office promptly and coordinate with other professionals you may work with, and our fee schedule is very competitive.*

Prospect: *I can appreciate that, but what I'm really getting at is what makes you tick. What's unique about you and your firm that would make me feel we have a good meeting of the minds here?*

Advisor: *Paul, I really love this business. I enjoy working with people and helping them solve their problems. I built the firm so we can provide comprehensive planning services for people like you who have complex needs.*

Prospect: *Okay, John, I do have another place where I need to be in 30 minutes, so what else can you tell me?*

Advisor (thinking to himself): This guy's already checked out of the conversation; what did I do wrong?

Plenty. The advisor made no connection whatsoever with the prospect. The whole conversation was delivered in generalities and went no deeper than surface level. It was like skipping stones on water. This prospect wanted more—and the advisor failed to deliver.

Let's look at a revised version of the above scenario. This time we'll assume the advisor has completed the Blueprinting process.

Prospect: *So, John, I'm here because Mike Smith suggested I meet with you. He knew I was unhappy with my current advisor, and he felt you could help me. What I'd like to know is what makes you different from my present advisor.*

Blueprinting advisor: *Well, Paul, I know there are many other advisors you could work with, but I believe what we're doing here and what we stand for is unique. Let me share something with you. When I was 16 years old, my father died of a heart attack. Unfortunately, he had only a small amount of insurance and we had few savings. For the next ten years, I watched my mother struggle as she tried to work full-time and raise three kids. Money was always tight, and we lived from paycheck to paycheck, but through her love and hard work we made it. Eventually, my mom remarried and the story has a happy ending, but that experience left an indelible mark on me. It gave me the desire and conviction to work with families to help them achieve financial peace of mind. I don't want other people to go through the struggle my family did, and I don't want people to lose what they already have.*

Prospect: *I can appreciate that. Your mom must be a saint.*

Blueprinting advisor: *She's pretty terrific, and she's a great role model for me on how to live life. As I watched my mom during those tough years, it became apparent to me that she was very clear on three things. First, taking care of our family was her number one priority. She made sure we had our basic material needs taken care of, and then she surrounded us with love. Second, she was very passionate about community service, and her passion got all us kids excited about it too. And third, she knew what she valued and what she cherished, and she lived those values.*

I know I'm telling you a lot about my mom and you may be wondering what this has to do with my business. Because of my mom's experience, I realized that my passion was to help people financially. If I could, through thoughtful financial planning, help people multiply their current savings and earnings as well as protect what they already have, then that would give me a great sense of satisfaction. I'd feel that I was making something good out of the struggle my mother went through. So I began my business with a simple mission—to help families build their wealth for the future and protect their present assets from the unforeseen.

My passion for helping families grow their wealth and protect their assets from the unforeseen, borne from my experience of growing up after my dad died unexpectedly, is what makes our firm unique.

Prospect: *I can see, John, that you feel very strongly about what you're doing here. What's our next step?*

Do you see the difference? The Blueprinting advisor never got into a discussion about service levels, consolidated statements, fee schedules, or any other generic business stuff. Yes, there's a time and a place for that discussion but not at the beginning of the conversation. The prospect wants to know that he or she is dealing with a competent, caring, thoughtful, trustworthy, and passionate advisor. If you can express that at the beginning of your conversation with the prospect, everything else will fall into place. But that type of conversation will only happen after you've spent some quality time reflecting, contemplating, and completing the Blueprinting exercises.

Values, meaningful purpose, mission statements sure sound like a lot of touchy-feely stuff, doesn't it? Well, folks, it is. Remember, you're advising people about some of the things that are dearest to them—money, protection, and legacy to name a few. You ought to know a thing or two about what makes you tick before you can accurately understand, interpret, and advise other people what they should do in these areas.

As you begin the Blueprinting exercises, it's important that you approach them with the proper frame of mind and that you find a quiet, conducive place to work. A cabin, your weekend home, or even a hotel room across town (yes, one of our coaching clients booked a hotel room for the weekend to get a good start on his exercises) can work.

The more serious you take these exercises, the more meaningful your results will be. By keeping an open mind, looking deep inside yourself to find your true thoughts, and not dismissing findings that don't fit your preconceived notions, you'll get results that will speed you on your way to personal and professional growth.

2

IDENTIFY AND LIVE
BY YOUR VALUES

*"Personal leadership is the process of keeping your vision and values before you
and aligning your life to be congruent with them."*
—STEPHEN COVEY

In August 2003, Geeta Anand of the *Wall Street Journal* wrote a story about John Crowley's struggle to save the life of his two children, Megan and Patrick. The kids were born with Pompe disease, a fatal illness that affects fewer than 10,000 people worldwide. Their prognosis was not good.

Moved to action, Crowley quit his job, leveraged his home, borrowed from his 401(k) plan, and started a biotech company with the goal of developing a cure for his kids. Eventually, he raised $27 million in venture capital. With early trials promising, he sold the company to Genzyme Corp. for $137 million in the hope that would help get the drug into testing and production much faster.

With hopes raised and dashed several times, Crowley was losing faith that he'd ever get a treatment to his ailing kids. Then, on Christmas Eve 2002, a letter arrived from a small hospital in New Jersey that said the hospital would perform a trial with Crowley's kids using the new experimental treatment developed by Genzyme. By the fall of 2003, Megan had shown significant improvement from use of the experimental drug whereas Patrick's improvement was limited.

This heart-wrenching story by Geeta Anand dramatically highlights the power of understanding your values and pursuing your meaningful purpose in life. John Crowley valued his kids and effectively risked everything to try to find a cure for their disease. Finding the cure became the meaningful purpose in his life. In the end, his dogged pursuit led to one of his kids getting significantly better while still holding out hope for the second child.

Fortunately, most of us don't have to experience this kind of heartache to illuminate the importance of living our values and pursuing our meaningful purpose.

WHAT ARE YOUR VALUES?

All of us have values. Values are the things that have intrinsic worth to us, the qualities that we hold dear and strive to live by. But most of the time we don't consciously think about what our values are.

Sometimes our values get out of whack. To see if yours are, take out a piece of paper and draw two vertical lines so you end up dividing the paper into three columns. In the left column, write down Recreation, Work, Family, Faith, and Fitness on separate rows. In the middle column, write down what percentage of your waking hours are spent in each of the five areas listed in the first column. In the third column, prioritize each of these areas on a scale of 1 to 5, with 1 being the most important and 5 the least important.

Now take a look at your list. Do you see any incongruities? Is there any area that you ranked as very important yet where you're only spending a small percentage of your time? The Values Clarification Exercise in Figure 2.1 expands this exercise, asking you to write down the six things that are most important to you and then rank them in order of priority. After you've completed your list, you can determine whether your day is spent doing and living those values.

WHY THINK ABOUT YOUR VALUES?

What are some of the benefits of consciously thinking about and living your values? First of all, it makes decision making a lot easier. We're confronted in life with tough choices all the time. Do I spend more time at work because I want to provide a good income for my family and give my family opportunities? Or do I spend more time with my family because that's important too, and I can live with a little less money? So we are always faced with these tough choices. But when we're clear about our values, making those choices is much, much easier.

Here's an example of how knowing your values makes decision making easier. In September 2002, a financial advisor, Greg, joined our Quest for Excellence Coaching Program. At the time, he was an average producer hoping our program could help take him to the next level. Well, we sure helped him. Six weeks after he joined, he sent Steve an e-mail saying he wanted to quit. So Steve called him and asked why he wanted to quit after such a short time in the program. Greg said it was because of the Blueprinting exercises that he had just completed. Intrigued, Steve asked him to elaborate. Greg said completing the Blueprinting exercises made him realize that his heart was not in this business. What he really valued was reaching college-age kids through public speaking, and it took completing the Values Clarification and other Blueprinting exercises to bring that point home. So he developed a plan to sell his practice over the next six months and move into public speaking full-time.

The Values Clarification Exercise helped Greg determine what was important to him. He became focused on what he valued, realized it wasn't in the financial planning business, and then developed a plan to move toward what he did value.

Don't get us wrong; we don't want all of you to follow Greg's path and get out of this business! But we do want you to consciously focus on what you value so that, as a result, your decision-making process will get easier.

Second, by knowing your values, you can consciously spend more time living those values. When you live your values, you're honoring yourself, and your life is aligned with the things that are most important to you. The more time you can spend doing, and living by, the things that are most important to you, the happier you're going to be. Think back to a time when you were happiest in your life. Maybe it was a family vacation, or a spiritual awakening, or time you spent with someone close to you. We'll bet at those times you were fully engaged in living your values.

Third, focusing on your values can give you the motivation to achieve. There are countless stories of people that have such strong convictions about their values that they were willing to be martyrs and give up their lives for that. Fortunately, you don't have to do that in our business, but when you have those strong convictions and those strong values, they give you the motivation and burning desire to really achieve.

CLARIFYING WHAT'S IMPORTANT TO YOU

As you reflect on your values, here are a few questions you can ask yourself that might help you clarify what's important to you.

First, what story inspired you or made a major impression on you? Stories are all around us. Some are funny. Some are educational. And some are so touching that they really strike a nerve with us. These touching stories are the ones that cause us to rethink who we are and what we're doing. They don't just affect us at a surface level; they penetrate our core and stay with us long after we first heard them. As you think about your story, delve into it and try to understand what it is about the story that moved you. When you look at it that way, you'll likely find some of your core values.

You may recall back in 1996 when a large group of mountain climbers ran into trouble while trying to summit Mount Everest. The story was made popular in a book called *Into Thin Air* by Jon Krakauer. Near the end of the day, a storm hit the mountain trapping some of the world's best climbers. One of these climbers, a New Zealander named Rob Hall, had just summited and was on his way down when the storm struck. Delirious and weak, he couldn't get down to camp and had to spend the night at more that 28,000 feet in a blizzard with a subzero temperature and no tent. As an expedition leader, he carried a two-way radio and through the magic of technology was patched through to his wife in New Zealand.

Imagine this scene. You're sitting near the top of the world's highest mountain all alone, a storm is raging, your legs and hands have frostbite, and you know you're going to die. With that backdrop, Hall began talking to his wife, who was at home pregnant with their first child. In this brief exchange overheard by several other climbers, Hall signed off by saying, "I love you. Sleep well, my sweetheart. Please don't worry too much." Days later Hall was found frozen to death. His body remains on Everest buried under the snow.

Stories like this point out the struggle between personal ambition and family desires. Rob Hall was doing what he loved to do, but he was in a very risky business—climbing the world's highest mountain—and also had a wife and a child on the way. There's a thin line between personal, selfish ambition and responsibility for those depending on you. The tragedy of Rob Hall, sitting on top of Mount Everest, freezing to death, and talking to his wife who's carrying his unborn child, is an example of a story that can put things in perspective very quickly.

Second, what event or occurrence moved you? It could be getting married or getting divorced. It could be the birth of a child or the death of a loved one. It could be a brush with death that put things in perspective for you. The effect on you is similar to the story above, but the difference is that this is something that happened to you, so it's much more real. You're more likely to change your behavior from an occurrence that happens to you compared with hearing a story that moves you. Either way, as you dig into the occurrence and try to understand its meaning to you, you'll likely find some of your core values.

Third, what's the secret to life that you would pass on to a future generation? If someone came up to you and said, "I want you to think about the one thing you learned in life that would be worthwhile for future generations to know," what would it be? By answering this question, you'll automatically describe what's important to you and what you value.

As you think about your values, it's also helpful to visualize what living those values looks and feels like. Your values shouldn't just be things you write on paper; rather, they should be in the form of verbs. For example, if health is important to you, then you should be lifting weights, doing cardio exercises, getting the right amount of sleep, and eating right. If you value good health but you're not doing any of the activities that promote good health, then good health is not a very strong value for you. If it were, you would find the time and energy to do the beneficial activities.

A great example of values in action occurred at the 1968 Olympics in Mexico City. African marathon runner John Aqwari started the race in great shape but by the 18th mile, he became dizzy and disoriented. He stumbled, fell to the ground, and banged his knee on the pavement. Not wanting to quit, he got up and started running again, but by now he was bleeding badly from his knee. His coach and the spectators along the route were yelling at him to stop. Ignoring their pleas, he kept shuffling along. About

45 minutes later, the race was officially over as the winner crossed the finish line.

But the race wasn't over for John Aqwari. More than an hour after the winner crossed the finish line, John Aqwari limped his way toward the Olympic Stadium, which was full of thousands of spectators busy watching other events. All of a sudden, from one end of the stadium a solitary figure came shuffling in with a bandaged leg and bleeding. The crowd didn't know how to react. The marathon had been over for a long time. Gradually, it began to dawn on the crowd that this guy was from the marathon and wanted to finish the race. And so as he started hobbling around the track, the applause started getting louder and louder and louder. And by the time he crossed that finish line, the applause was a thunderous roar. Aqwari then collapsed from exhaustion and was taken to the hospital.

While he was at the hospital, one of the reporters asked him, "Mr. Aqwari, why didn't you just drop out of the race? Why did you keep going after you were in such obvious pain?" Aqwari looked at him straight in the eye and said, "My country did not send me 6,000 miles to start the race; they sent me to finish the race."

Aqwari was very clear what his values were. It was critically important that he represent his country well and finish what he had started. He didn't want to let his countrymen down. They had spent a lot of money to get him there, and he wanted to show them that they had made a good choice. He also clearly had a burning desire. He saw the finish line and wasn't going to let anything stop him from reaching it. It was a true example of values in action.

Our values can be viewed as a continuum with things of great value on the left and things of no value or even negative value on the right. As you look at the right side of the continuum, it's filled with things that cause us discomfort or pain. For example, we have a coaching client who detests negative people. One day he called us about a staffing issue. He explained that for the past nine years, he's had an employee named Marge who does good work, connects well with the clients, but fills the office with a negative attitude. Our coaching client didn't even like going to his own office anymore because of the "negativity" Marge brought to the work environment. Our client kept Marge on staff for so many years because she did good work, and the hassle of replacing her would seem to require more effort than just putting up with her. Our advice to our client: "Marge has got to go."

Imagine how much better off our client would have been had he let Marge go nine years ago instead of letting her hang around and fill the office with a negative aura. If something is causing you discomfort and it's within your power to change it—then change it.

Take a look at your life right now. Are there any negative values that are taking up an inordinate amount of your time? Make a conscious effort to move away from what causes you pain and discomfort and toward those values that bring you happiness and closer to your goals. Schedule some quiet time to complete the Values Clarification Exercise in Figure 2.1.

If you're married, have your spouse complete this exercise too. When you're done, compare and discuss your results. If your values diverge, it's time to have a deep conversation. If you share similar values, find ways that you can help each other reinforce them. This simple exercise can be richly rewarding for the two of you.

If you have young kids, you've probably heard the phrase, "Mom, can I have a cookie?" or "Dad, can I have a cookie?" It seems that giving them a cookie is all it takes to make kids happy. Adults are like that too except our cookies are a little different. Instead of being made of flour, sugar, eggs, vanilla, butter, and chocolate chips, our cookies are expensive material things. Our cookies are nice homes, expensive cars, fancy vacations, or bigger commission checks. When kids get their cookie, they're happy.

FIGURE 2.1 *Values Clarification Exercise*

In this exercise, you'll identify what you value most in life and then rank them from most important to least important. Examples that might appear on your list include: family, health, spiritual fulfillment, love, relationships, generosity, adventure, achievement, passion, leaving a legacy, fun/happiness, creativity, positive attitude, helping others, financial security, learning, peace of mind, fame, respect, and personal growth.

Directions: List six things you value most in life and then rank them in order of importance to you.

The things I value most in life are:

Rank Value

But for adults, getting a cookie doesn't always make them happy. Sometimes, once we have our cookie, it begins to crumble. We start to get concerned about keeping our cookie or protecting our cookie from other people. We realize that our cookie may make us happy in one aspect of our life, but it adds new problems and complexity in another area of our life.

And so we start spending more of our time trying to protect our cookie than really enjoying it. As you go through life, we think you'll realize that having the cookie is really not what life or happiness is all about. You'll get the most from your life by spending your time engaged in the activities you enjoy and surrounding yourself with the people you love. The Values Clarification Exercise helps you hone in on what those values are so you can develop a plan to spend more time living them.

SUMMARY

- Values are the things that have intrinsic worth to us. These are the qualities that we hold dear and strive to live.
- The benefits of consciously thinking about and living your values include the following:
  - Decision making becomes a lot easier.
  - By knowing your values, you can consciously spend more time living those values, and that in turn will increase your happiness.
  - Focusing on your values can give you the motivation to achieve.
- By answering the following questions, you can help clarify what's important to you:
  - What story inspired you or made a major impression on you?
  - What event or occurrence moved you?
  - What's the secret to life that you would pass on to a future generation?
- Ask your spouse to complete the Values Clarification Exercise too and compare results. By knowing each other's values, you can deepen your relationship.

3

FIND YOUR
MEANINGFUL PURPOSE

"We are not here merely to make a living. We are here to enrich the world."
—WOODROW WILSON

Once you understand what's important to you, you can start thinking about your meaningful purpose. In fact, at Peak Productions we think finding, or for many of you rediscovering, your meaningful purpose is one of the most important things you can do. Meaningful purpose is your compelling reason for being, and if we can help you find it through this book or through our coaching program, then we think we've succeeded.

We believe that all of us are here for a reason and that reason is something greater than ourselves. We all have certain desires and pursuits in life, such as ensuring our security and caring for loved ones. But when you move beyond the day-to-day pursuits of life, what moves you? What causes you to jump out of bed in the morning feeling refreshed and ready to tackle the day's challenges? What higher purpose calls you?

Jay Earley, PhD, defines meaningful purpose as "a contribution to the world that uses your whole self fully and gives your life passion, fulfillment, and meaning through dedication to something larger than yourself." Without meaningful purpose, we simply go through the motions of daily life. We respond to the alarm clock, we go to work, we solve the day's problems, we eat, we relax, we go to bed, and then we wake up and do it all over again. We could do that for 50 years and then look back on what we've accomplished and be sadly disappointed at how much time we spent accomplishing so little.

Meaningful purpose transcends what we do for ourselves and reaches out to the world around us and infuses life with the special gifts that each of us have inside. Your meaningful purpose does not have to necessarily change the world. It could be something very close to home such as raising kids who become productive members of society. It could be bringing love and kindness to neglected people in our society. It could just be living each day with a positive attitude and bringing a little joy to somebody else's world.

On the other hand . . . your meaningful purpose may involve trying to change the world. Regardless of the magnitude of your impact, knowing what your meaningful purpose is will go a long way toward bringing passion and enthusiasm into your life.

If you're having trouble thinking about what your meaningful purpose is, try writing your eulogy. That's right; start at the end and work backward. Imagine your funeral is taking place and you're hovering above the grieving guests observing the scene. Your casket is near the front, and your best friend is standing in the pulpit eulogizing. What is he or she saying about you and your life? More important, what do you *want* your best friend to say about you and your life?

Kind of scary, huh? As you continue to observe the scene from your warm spot near the ceiling, how many true friends can you spot in the audience? How many people did you connect with in your life that would go the distance for you and be there for you at the drop of a hat? If you have one or two true friends like that, then you have one or two more than most people. Many of us go through life developing a large number of acquaintances but very few true friends. What can you do in your remaining years to develop true friendships?

Also ask yourself, what will people remember about me 100 years from now? What lasting legacy will I leave? Your material goods will be long gone, and what will remain are the lives of the people you've touched—your family, your descendants, and other people with whom you've shared your generosity. So think about that. What can you do in the rest of your life that will still be positively remembered 100 years from now? The answer may cause you to change what you're doing today.

You'll know you've got your eulogy just right when reading it gets you all choked up. Don't be bashful. Nobody has to read this eulogy right now except you. Dream a little. Stretch a little. Look deep inside and ask yourself what you are really here to do. What do you want to accomplish that will give your life significance? Writing your eulogy is a great way to look back on your life and figure out, while you still have time, what it is you want to do that will have a lasting impact. Knowing and pursuing your purpose can also help you live longer.

During World War II, psychologist Victor Frankl was sent to a concentration camp. While there, he tried to figure out a way to survive that horrible period. He noticed that among those who were given a chance to survive, it was those who found meaning and a reason to live who were more likely to make it through. These were the people who found a purpose they could cling to, whether it was staying alive so they could be reunited with a loved one or staying alive so they could accomplish a task. Frankl did survive the concentration camp, and he spent the rest of his life devoted to helping others find their meaningful purpose. By the time he died in 1997, Frankl had written more than 25 books, had developed a new branch of psychology, and had become one of the century's great thinkers.

Finding your meaningful purpose may not be a life-sustaining necessity as it was for Dr. Frankl, but its effect on you could be just as powerful.

WHERE DO YOU FIND MEANINGFUL PURPOSE?

Here's a little quiz for you. Try to guess the author of the following quotation:

"All men seek one goal, success or happiness. The only way to achieve true success is to express yourself completely in service to society."

You may be surprised to learn that these words were spoken by Aristotle. For more than 2,000 years, people have been thinking about success and happiness. Success and happiness are really about contributing, according to Aristotle, and that's about something outside of yourself.

More recently, John Templeton said, "Think less about what you can get and more about what you can give, and your life may take on a luster you never dreamed possible." Similarly to Aristotle, Templeton contends purpose is about contributing, about helping other people. When you step outside of yourself, as suggested by such diverse thinkers as Aristotle and Templeton, that's where you're going to find your meaningful purpose.

Some of you may find meaningful purpose in your work as a financial advisor. Some of you may find it outside of work. Although work is not the be-all and end-all, you nevertheless should find some meaning from it. If not, then you've got two options.

First, you could leave the business and find another one more to your liking. Or second, you could restructure your business operation and make it more meaningful.

To make your business more meaningful, figure out which aspects of the business appeal to you and then focus on them. In this book, we'll tell you the specific things you need to do to build a $1 million practice; if you follow them, you'll get there with no doubt about it. But if building your practice the way we describe is not compatible with your passion and your meaningful purpose, then you'll be no happier with a $1 million practice than you are with a $100,000 practice. Build your business in a way that's compatible with who you are and what you're trying to accomplish.

Here's the key insight we want you to remember: *leverage your passion.* Find your meaningful purpose because when you have purpose, you have passion. Then structure your business to leverage your passion so you can confidently strive toward your meaningful purpose. When you do that, your business and your life will soar.

The Meaningful Purpose Exercise in Figure 3.1 will help you discover your meaningful purpose and set you on a path toward pursuing it.

SUMMARY

- All of us are here for a reason, and that reason is something greater than ourselves. Meaningful purpose transcends what we do for ourselves and reaches out to the world around us and infuses life with the special gifts that each of us has inside.
- If you're having trouble deciding what your meaningful purpose is, try writing your eulogy.
- Knowing and pursuing your purpose can help you live longer.
- To make your business more meaningful, figure out what aspects of the business appeal to you and then focus on them.
- If building your practice the way we describe is not compatible with your passion and your meaningful purpose, then

FIGURE 3.1 *Meaningful Purpose Exercise*

The following questions are designed to help you identify, unlock, and pursue your meaningful purpose so the world can benefit from your unique gifts. Your objective is to reflect on them, write your response, and then consciously decide how you are going to move forward in living your life with meaningful purpose.

1. Imagine your funeral is taking place, and your spirit is hovering above the grieving guests observing the scene. Your casket is near the front and your best friend is standing in the pulpit eulogizing. Write down what you would like your best friend to say in your eulogy.

2. Think about the last time you really felt fulfilled in your life. What were you doing?

3. Have you ever had a hunger to do something for other people that is totally different from your day-to-day existence? For example, maybe you saw a TV show about orphan children in Russia, and you felt moved to do something. Or maybe you feel compelled to reduce obesity in our society by promoting the benefits of healthy living. Write down what you had (or have) a hunger to do for other people even if you think it's totally impractical.

4. What do you value most in life? (Restate your top values from Figure 2.1)

5. What are you most passionate about?

6. What's the one thing you could do that meets all the following criteria?
   a. It's so important to you that you would want your best friend to mention it in your eulogy.
   b. You are fulfilled when doing it.
   c. It feeds a hunger that you have.
   d. It is compatible with your highest values.
   e. You are passionate about it.

Your answer to question 6 is where you'll find your meaningful purpose in life.

you'll be no happier with a $1 million practice than you are with a $100,000 practice.

- Build your business in a way that's compatible with who you are and what you're trying to accomplish.

4

DEVELOP A COMPELLING VISION FOR YOUR FUTURE

*"Your vision will become clear only when you look into your heart.
Who looks outside dreams. Who looks inside awakens."*

—CARL JUNG

You may be more of a visionary than you think according to a recent example from Steve.

Not long ago I asked Patrick, one of our coaching clients, how he was coming along on developing his compelling vision for the future. Patrick said, "I'm just not that kind of guy. When you talk about that stuff, I'm the one in the back of the room trying to hide. It's just not my nature to think in those terms."

So I asked him, "What kind of practice do you want?" Boy, did he light up. He spent the next few minutes outlining exactly what his business looked like, where his office was located, who his clients were, how his staff was structured, how much his revenue was, how much time he was taking off, how he was spending his free time, and so on. I said, "Patrick, that's your compelling vision. You're so excited telling me about it because I asked you. Imagine if you had it written down and looked at it each morning as you got ready for work! Do you think your day would be more exciting and your results more significant?" He got the point.

Your compelling vision is a vivid description of your ideal life. It's a written narrative that highlights the kind of life you want to live. You may never ultimately reach this ideal life and that's okay. What you're doing is setting the bar high and giving yourself something to aim for. If you aim for the stars and just make it to the moon, you've still made it farther than almost everybody else.

Here's an example of a compelling vision for the future.

I enthusiastically jump out of bed every morning full of energy and excitement for the day ahead. Through my daily activities, I am a husband my wife is proud of, a father my children look up to, and a friend people count on.

My family is financially secure, physically fit, and emotionally close. We live in a comfortable home on one acre with a postcard-perfect view of the Pacific Ocean. Our home is light and airy with crisp ocean breezes blowing through. Pictures of my family and special moments in our life line the walls. The sound of grandchildren fills the house. As I look out the window, I see waves lapping the shore, seals playing on the rocks, and surfers hanging ten.

My days are spent helping the people around me reach their fullest potential. I do this by meeting with my top 75 clients (all of whom have at least $1 million invested with me), guiding them in reaching their dreams and aspirations, and delivering advice that creates financial peace of mind. I have an office that's just ten minutes from my home; it's trimmed with fine wood, has my collection of modern art lining the walls, and is a place that makes me, my staff, and my clients feel at home and very comfortable.

My outstanding staff of five and my highly systematized office allows me to work only four days a week and take eight weeks of vacation every year. For enjoyment, my wife and I travel the world, kick back at our second home in the desert, visit our kids and grandkids, read, and take time to enjoy the beauty of the great outdoors.

When I go to bed at night, I sleep soundly knowing that I helped make the world a little better than when I woke up.

You have a blank canvas in front of you and it's called your future. You can make that future happen any way you want it to. But first you have to know what you want that future to be. That's why we want you to write a compelling vision that pulls you toward it, that gives you something to strive for and pursue.

As you read your compelling vision each morning, it should fill you with energy and enthusiasm. It should be extremely motivational and give you the impetus you need to start each day with purpose, passion, and direction.

DEVELOPING YOUR COMPELLING VISION OF THE FUTURE

Merriam-Webster's Collegiate Dictionary (11th ed.) defines vision as "a supernatural appearance that conveys a revelation." How appropriate. "Supernatural" is defined as outside of the visible, observable world. It suggests there's some other force at work here. That "other force" is your subconscious mind. By having a compelling vision and reading it each morning, you're hard-wiring your brain to focus on that vision and work toward making it happen—even when you're not consciously thinking about it. "Appearance," of course, is something you can see. When you have a vision, your mind develops a picture of that vision, and it throws your body into overdrive to make it happen.

"Conveys a revelation" suggests a foretelling of something that's about to happen. By having that compelling vision and having a picture of that vision in your mind's eye, your body will mobilize to take action and to do the things that are necessary to get you closer and closer to achieving it.

Your compelling vision is inextricably linked to your definition of success. We all know the media have their definition of success—how much money and toys you can accumulate. For example, *Forbes* magazine has its annual ranking of the 400 richest people in the world, and Robin Leach used to give us a titillating view of the *Lifestyles of the Rich and Famous.* We're all fascinated by wealth and material goods, but deep down we know that that's not really a good definition of success.

So how do you define success? The truth is, there is no one definition of success. It's personal. It's different for each person. There are however, a few principles that permeate the life of successful people. They're living their values. They're doing what gives them purpose. They're surrounded by the people they love. Knowing what success means to you will make writing your compelling vision a smoother process.

There's an old story about a pastor who had an obsession with golf.

> Early one Sunday as he was getting ready for church, the pastor realized what a beautiful, glorious day it was going to be. Overcome by the golfing bug, he called his assistant pastor and asked him to take over because he was too sick to preach. With the worship service covered, he plopped his clubs in the trunk and took off for a golf course far away where nobody would recognize him.
>
> Observing from up above, an angel turned to God and said, "God, do you see what he's doing?" "Of course" said God. The angel said, "God, shouldn't we punish him for this bad judgment?" God answered, "Yes." So God and the angel watched the pastor as he proceeded to par the first hole, birdie the second and third holes, par the fourth, and eagle the fifth. This

phenomenal round of golf continued until the 18th hole. The angel then turned to God and said, "God, I thought you said we should punish him; instead, he's shooting the best round of golf in his life, and he's only got one hole left to play." God said not to worry.

On the 18th hole, which was a short but tricky downhill par 4, the pastor took out his driver, addressed the ball, and gave it a huge whack. Just then, a strong gust of wind came up and literally propelled the ball to just short of the green where it bounced twice, rolled 30 feet and dropped straight into the cup for a hole in one. Incredulous, the angel turned to God and said, "I can't believe this; the pastor skipped Sunday worship, played golf instead, shoots the best round of golf in his life, and caps it off with a hole in one. I don't understand how this is punishment."

God looked at the angel and said, "Who can he tell it to?"

Success is not about being selfish. Success is better when it can be shared. Knowing what success means to you will help you develop your compelling vision of the future.

CREATE A PICTURE OF YOUR COMPELLING VISION

Helen Keller was deaf and blind from the age of two. Someone once asked her, "What would be worse than being born blind?" She replied, "To have sight but no vision." Everybody reading this book has sight, but not everybody has vision. As you create your compelling vision of the future, go beyond just writing it down. Try to fix a picture of it in your mind.

It helps to train yourself to think like a photojournalist. A photojournalist tries to take that one snapshot that truly captures the essence of a decisive moment in time or in history. In one picture, a photojournalist can evoke all kinds of feelings and emotions that completely summarize a situation and freeze them in our minds. The picture tells a whole story and is literally a picture that's worth a thousand words.

Remember the picture of little John Kennedy Jr. saluting as his father's casket rolled by back in November 1963? How about the picture of Neil Armstrong standing on the moon looking at the American flag or the lone Chinese man standing in front of the tank in Tiananmen Square? And, most recently, the poignant picture of the New York firemen raising the American flag on top of the twin towers' debris on 9/11 is forever etched in our memory.

Each of those pictures tells a complete story and engenders a full range of emotions. Little John brings back memories of that fateful day when the nation mourned the loss of its youthful president. Neil Armstrong standing on the moon capped a decade-long challenge to beat the Russians and fulfill John Kennedy's vision to put a man on the moon by the end of the decade. The defiant Chinese reminded us that we can all make a difference. And the New York firemen reminded us that even in the midst of utter destruction, there is still hope in all that makes America great.

As you think about your compelling vision, try to create in your mind a picture like those above that totally encapsulates the scene. What does the environment look like? What are you doing? Who are you surrounded by? How are you feeling? Once your picture comes into focus, call it up frequently and use it to keep yourself motivated and on track.

Perhaps the best visualizers are athletes. No doubt you've seen a professional golfer go through his or her preshot routine and look down the fairway to visualize the ball flying through its intended trajectory. Or Olympic divers standing still on the high platform as they go through in their minds every twist and turn on their way to the water ten meters below. The night before the high school state track meet, Steve sat in the top row of the stadium and visualized himself running all eight laps and crossing the finish line in first place. The next day, that vision came true. Athletes know that every great achievement happens twice—once in their minds and once in reality.

When was the last time you put a jigsaw puzzle together without looking at the picture? Pretty tough, isn't it? Then why would you leave your future to random happenstance when you can create a picture of it and then put the pieces in place to make it happen? Developing that picture helps connect everything inside you and energizes your body to make that vision a reality.

MAKE IT COMPELLING

In 1963, Dr. Martin Luther King stood at the foot of the Lincoln Memorial in front of 250,000 people and electrified this audience. With full passion and conviction, he said . . . "I have a dream . . ." He used rich imagery and vivid language to mobilize not just the audience to take action but millions of people across the country. As a result, our country made major changes to its civil rights. Dr. King had a compelling vision for the future; he acted on it and brought about massive change.

On a smaller scale, Steve Jobs of Apple Computer relied on a vision to recruit John Sculley to join the company in the early 1980s. At the time, Sculley was working for Pepsico. In the critical moment, as the two were walking through the Stanford University campus, Jobs turned to Sculley and said, "Do you want to sell sugar water the rest of your life, or do you want to change the world?" Jobs's vision was too much to resist.

Paul and Linda McCartney had a wonderful vision for their family. After Linda died, Paul explained in an interview how they had a vision for their family. He said that in their 30 years of marriage, they spent only 11 nights apart. Those were the 11 nights that he was in jail on drug charges in Japan involving marijuana, so he really had no choice. Other than that, they made an effort to be together even though Paul traveled the world.

Paul went on to say that they lived in London early in their marriage, but because they didn't want their kids to be exposed to the trappings of the big city, they moved to the country. They also didn't want their kids raised by nannies, so Paul and Linda took turns taking their kids to and from school. And when Linda died, Paul made sure it was a special family event. As famous as he was, he didn't invite politicians or dignitaries to the funeral. He just wanted people who meant something to the family; as a result, Yoko Ono was out and the pilot of their plane was in. And in her last days, Linda spent her time in Santa Barbara, California, because that was a part of the country that she liked and where she felt comfortable. Together, Paul and Linda McCartney had a great vision that lasted 30 years.

Famous people aren't the only ones who have a vision. In the early 1990s, Musashi Case was a 27-year-old architect living in Hawaii and making $200,000 a year. At the time, he was doing some design work for the Four Seasons Hotel when he hooked up with Jack Nicklaus, who was designing a golf course on the property. As he got to know Nicklaus, he became totally inspired about golf. Back then, Case was playing golf only about four times a year, but something inside Case made him decide that his vision for the future was to become a professional golfer. So against his parents' wishes he quit his job, and for the next ten years he did nothing but play golf. Sadly, he never won a tournament, never made a cut, and, in fact, never made a penny playing golf. He travels the country in a beat-up old car and gets free rent from a friend.

Why does he do it? During a tournament stop in Omaha in 2001, Case told a reporter from the *Omaha World-Herald* that "everyone thinks I'm crazy, but this is my dream. I don't care whether I go broke or not; when I'm 65 I can tell myself that I tried." He has a vision that he's pursuing. He may never reach it, but at least he'll never have any regrets.

As you think about your vision, you will never be greater than the vision guides you, so think big. You may never reach your vision, but that's okay because it gives you something to strive for. Look at Southwest Airlines. Its vision is to make the cost of flying as inexpensive as the cost of driving. It may never get there, but it is striving toward that vision. Early in its history, Microsoft's vision was to have a personal computer on every desktop running Microsoft software. It's come close and keeps pushing toward it.

Your vision sets the bar high—and gives you something to strive toward. And as you move toward it, your business, your life, your mission, and your values all need to be aligned so there's no incongruity.

Figure 4.1 contains the Compelling Vision Exercise, which is a series of thought-provoking questions. Answering these questions truthfully will make your compelling vision come into clear focus. Here are a few we'd like to elaborate:

1. My ideal working environment is . . . ?
   Where we live and work is a critical part of our vision. Are you comfortable in your present geographic location? Do you long to live somewhere else? What do your ideal surroundings look like? What does your office look like? What pictures do you have on the wall? Do you have some meaningful things in there that are important to you?

2. I want to spend my days working on . . . ?
   During an interview, Steve once asked a candidate what his ideal day looked like. After 15 seconds of silence, the candidate said something very profound: "I don't know." No wonder he was unemployed. Ask yourself, what am I doing from the moment I get up in the morning to the moment I go to bed at night that's going to give me energy and make me feel passionate and enthusiastic?

3. If I weren't so afraid I would . . . ?
   Nike states it so eloquently: "Just do it." Sometimes we have to push our limits in order to grow. We have to step in and out of our comfort zone. We've got to take those chances

to find our character and our limits to move forward and move toward the vision we're trying to reach.

4. My life will not be complete unless I . . . ?

What are some of the things that you've really got to do in this lifetime to make you feel good about what you've accomplished? It could be anything. It could be a religious pilgrimage. It could be getting close with someone you're estranged from. And if you know what that is today, what's stopping you from doing it or moving toward it?

5. If I had all the money I ever needed, I would spend the rest of my life . . . ?

Answer this one and you'll find where your passion lies. So often we get caught up thinking we need to make X amount of money to fulfill our dreams and desires. Under closer examination, you may find that what brings you happiness may actually be well within your reach.

6. I know it seems impossible, but my practice would improve dramatically if . . . ?

Until May of 1953, many people thought that it was physically impossible to run a mile in less than four minutes or to reach the summit of Mount Everest. Yet within 12 months, both had been accomplished. Once Roger Bannister broke the four-minute mile, dozens of people quickly followed him. It was the same thing with Mount Everest. Fifteen expeditions before Sir Edmund Hillary's had tried to reach the summit and failed; and some climbers died. After Hillary and Tenzing Norgay reached the top, the door flew open. In 2001, in fact, 88 people reached the summit—in one day!

So once the limiting beliefs were shattered, the floodgates opened. Ask yourself, Is there a limiting belief in my practice or my life? Chances are it is something that you can break through, overcome, and achieve.

By answering the questions in the Compelling Vision Exercise in Figure 4.1, you'll be able to pull your thoughts together and develop a vision that draws you toward it and keeps you enthusiastic day after day.

FIGURE 4.1 *Compelling Vision Exercise*

In this exercise, you'll paint a picture of your compelling vision. Don't hold back. Answer each question as accurately and completely as possible. This is your future, so make it a great one.

My ideal working environment is . . .

    Location . . .

    Surroundings . . .

The relationships I want to surround myself with are . . .

I want to spend my days working on . . .

(continued)

FIGURE 4.1 *Compelling Vision Exercise, continued*

If I weren't so afraid, I would . . .

My life will not be complete unless I . . .

If I had only six months to live, I would . . .

If I had all the money I ever needed, I would spend the rest of my life . . .

I want people to remember me by saying I was . . .

I feel alive and energetic after I have just . . .

FIGURE 4.1 *Compelling Vision Exercise, continued*

The community/world issue that I feel most strongly about is . . .

I know it seems impossible, but my practice would dramatically improve if . . .

Review how you answered all the previous questions. From this, write a Compelling Vision that motivates you to take action and that gives you great excitement from just thinking about it.

My Compelling Vision is to . . .

Surround myself with . . .

Live in . . .

Spend my days . . .

Accomplish . . .

SUMMARY

- Your compelling vision is a vivid description of your ideal life. It's a written narrative that highlights the kind of life you want to live. You may never ultimately reach this ideal life, but that's okay. What you're doing is setting the bar high and giving yourself something to aim for.

- As you read your compelling vision each morning, it should fill you with energy and enthusiasm. It should be extremely motivational and give you the impetus you need to start each day with purpose, passion, and direction.

- As you think about your compelling vision, try to create a picture in your mind that totally encapsulates the scene. What does the environment look like? What are you doing? Who are you surrounded by? How are you feeling? Once your picture comes into focus, call it up frequently and use it to keep you motivated and on track.

- Your vision sets the bar high and gives you something to strive toward. As you move toward it, your business, your life, your mission, and your values all need to be aligned so there's no incongruity.

5

DEVELOP A PERSONAL AND PROFESSIONAL MISSION STATEMENT

"Make your life a mission—not an intermission."
—ARNOLD GLASGOW

Once you know your compelling vision for the future, you need to develop a road map to get there. That's the personal mission statement. Your personal mission statement is a declaration of living. It describes the kind of person you want to be and the kind of life you want to live. It's your road map for daily living.

Your personal mission statement should become a part of who you are. You want to be able to look at it and say this is exactly who I am and what I stand for. It should give you a positive buzz without drugs. And when you get to that point, you'll know you've got a mission statement that connects with your very core and is meaningful to you.

But don't be content to let your personal mission statement collect dust over time. As you evolve, so too should your personal mission statement. What's important to you today may not be as important tomorrow. Life has a way of intervening and causing us to rethink our priorities from time to time, and, as that happens, your personal mission should be modified too.

A meaningful personal mission statement can help you weather the difficult times that we all face in our life. If your mission statement truly reflects what you believe in with every fiber of your being, then it's going to help you persevere during stormy weather.

DEVELOPING YOUR PERSONAL MISSION STATEMENT

Gleaning wisdom from our elders can be a great aid in helping you develop your personal mission statement. Richard Leider, founder of The Inventure Group, has spent many years talking to senior citizens and asking them what they would have done differently in their life. In a February 1998 *Fast Company* magazine article titled "Are You Deciding on Purpose?" Leider shared some of the conclusions he had drawn from these conversations.

First of all, these elderly people said they'd have been more reflective. They would have consciously taken more time to just step back from life and consider what it was they were doing and whether they were on the right road. Frequently, they found themselves getting so caught up in the "stuff" of daily life that they ended up just going through the motions and not having any real meaning attached to what they were doing. For many of them, it wasn't until a crisis occurred that they really stepped back and took the time to review their life and gain perspective.

Too often we get so busy in life that we become reactive instead of proactive. To change that, consider pulling your calendar out and actually scheduling time to do nothing but think. Think about your business. Think about your life. Do a gut check. If you don't schedule this reflective time, it's unlikely to ever happen on its own.

Second, these elderly people said time is precious. They realized that as they got older, time seemed to go much, much faster. They wished that they would have spent more time to stop and smell the roses. Think for a moment; as you hurry through life, are you passing by more than you're catching up to? Kids do a great job of stopping and smelling the roses. They get excited about everything because everything is new to them. This sense of wonderment tends to go away as we get older and that's unfortunate. Put yourself in a child's frame of mind sometime and take a second look at things that you would normally pass by. There are little miracles all around us if we just notice them instead of taking them for granted.

Third, senior citizens said that they would have taken more risks. They would have been more courageous in relationships and taken more creative chances. In the poem *The Voiceless,* Oliver Wendell Holmes wrote:

"A few can touch the magic string and noisy fame is proud to win them. Alas for those who never sing and die with all their music in them."

Our belief is that everybody has some God-given talents and gifts. Some of you are going to take those talents and gifts to your grave because of fear or a simple lack of motivation. And not only is that a tragedy for you, it's a tragedy for the world. Imagine if everybody in the world were contributing to society at their highest level? How different would life be? By challenging yourself to be courageous and take chances, you can unlock the door to your innate gifts and infuse the world with your spirit.

And fourth, the elderly said they would have made the effort to really understand what brought them fulfillment. In the *Fast Company* article, Leider wrote:

Fulfillment comes from realizing your talents, adding value and living by your values. Fulfillment comes from integrity, from being who you are and expressing who you are as fully as possible. It doesn't have to do with your job description or the specifics of your work. It has to do with how you bring yourself to your work, regardless of what that work is.

A cable network called HGTV used to air a show called *The Good Life* that was about people who had jumped out of the rat race and pursued their dream. They found their fulfillment and meaningful purpose by heeding their inner calling. One of the profiled guests gave up a legal career to open a small museum in Wisconsin. Another gave up a job as a plant manager in a family business to open a raspberry farm. And a third left a computer repair business to open a kayak retail store and give kayaking tours.

At the end of each show, the host asked each guest, "How do you define the good life?" And almost invariably, each would say the same thing. First, they're living where they want to live and where they feel "at home." Second, they're surrounded by the people they love. And, third, they're doing work that they enjoy and that gives them purpose.

It all seems so simple doesn't it? How close are you to living *your* good life? Are you living in a place that feels like home? Are you surrounded by the people you love? Are you doing work that you are passionate about and that gives you purpose? If you're not living your good life, how can you expect to help your clients reach theirs?

You'll get a good start on writing your personal mission statement by answering these four questions:

1. My mission is to . . . (Ask yourself what you really want to do in your life and what you want to accomplish.)
2. I value . . . (Earlier we went through a Values Clarification Exercise. Now you can reflect on what's important to you and tie that into your personal mission.)
3. I would like to contribute to . . . (Remember, your greatest satisfaction will come from shedding your selfishness and then reaching out to those around you. This isn't about

what's in it for me. Rather, ask yourself how you can contribute to your family, your church, your community, and society?)

4. My favorite motivational statement is . . . (You can end your personal mission statement with a motivational message that has special meaning to you.)

Keep in mind there's no set length to a personal mission statement. It could be just a sentence or two or a few paragraphs. However, it needs to be something that you can remember and that becomes part and parcel of who you are.

In addition to a personal mission statement, take it a step further by developing a joint mission statement with your spouse. The time you two will spend sharing your thoughts and desires as a couple can have a profoundly positive effect on your marriage. Knowing that you and your spouse are moving forward in life united behind a joint mission statement will enrich your relationship far beyond the surface level.

DEVELOPING A PROFESSIONAL MISSION STATEMENT

So far we've homed in on our values, discovered our meaningful purpose, developed a compelling vision for our future, and created a personal mission statement. Now we can develop a professional mission statement that is congruent with our personal needs. Much of what we talked about with the personal mission statement is applicable to the professional mission statement. This is simply your business road map. It's your calling card and your signature that clarifies why you are in business, what you stand for, and how you assist people.

It's helpful to get your staff involved with this one. You want them to feel good about it and have some equity in it. If they have a part in shaping it, they'll feel more compelled to live by it and exemplify it day in and day out.

Don't be bashful about sharing it with your clients either. The more they know about what makes you and your business tick, the more likely they are to develop a connective relationship that transcends a bull market. They'll stick with you through thick and thin if they believe in your mission and see you living it on a daily basis. You can share your mission with your clients in person, on your stationery, in your client newsletter, at your client events, and any other place that you feel is appropriate.

By completing the following five phrases, you'll have a good start on writing your business mission statement:

1. My company . . . (In a concise sentence, describe what your company does.)

2. We believe in . . . (Clients want to know that you have deeply held convictions about your business. Here's your chance to share them. For example, you may believe that asset allocation and diversification are the best ways to achieve financial security. Whatever it is you believe strongly in, share it!)

3. We serve . . . (Ask yourself who can benefit the most from your services and with whom you want to work. Your business mission statement can serve to attract those you want to work with and persuade those who don't fit your profile to look elsewhere.)

4. We exist . . . (Give your clients a compelling reason to work with you. They've got lots of choices because we're in a commodity business. Your job is to give them a compelling enough reason to convince them to do business specifically with you.)

5. Clients can expect . . . (You need to deliver results. Here's where you describe the services you offer, the "experience" clients will receive, and the results they can expect. Nobody

wants to do business with you without knowing what to expect.)

We've worked with advisors over the years who have been tempted to copy their mission and vision statements from other advisors. Their logic is that "it says what I want to say and I couldn't have said it better." Unfortunately, our experience shows that copying your mission or vision statement or modeling it after somebody else's doesn't work. You then become a "me too" advisor. You have no point of differentiation.

The main objective of developing a mission statement is to create one that totally resonates with you. It has to encapsulate your hopes, dreams, and aspirations for the way you want to live your life and the way you want to run your business. Chances are slim that somebody else out there wants to live the exact kind of life and run the exact kind of business that you do. We're all too unique for that to happen.

Another key reason for having a very personalized mission and vision is that they will help you deeply connect with your clients. When you can clearly articulate what you stand for and what makes you different, clients will be attracted to you. Clients want to work with people who have clear and deeply held beliefs and convictions. When you've got your mission and vision "right" for you, your passion, commitment, and authenticity will shine through, and clients will be drawn to that.

Be aware that this is a time-consuming process. It's not something you're going to knock off in a weekend. You'll go through drafts, sleep on it, make modifications, and eventually arrive at a point when you can say, "That's it, that's who I am, that's what I stand for, and that's why I'm in this business."

Now, as life goes on, you go through changes, mature, and gain wisdom. This means your "perfect" mission and vision today may not completely resonate with you five or ten years from now. Over time, if you feel your mission and vision are no longer connecting with you as they once did, it's time for a tune-up. As you evolve, they should evolve too.

SUMMARY

- Your personal mission statement is a declaration of living. It describes the kind of person you want to be and the kind of life you want to live. It's your road map for daily living.
- Your personal mission statement should become a part of who you are. You want to be able to look at it and say that this is exactly who I am and what I stand for. It should give you a positive buzz without drugs. Once you get to that point, you'll know you've got a mission statement that connects with your very core and is meaningful to you.
- There's no set length to a personal mission statement. It could be just a few sentences or a few paragraphs. However, it needs to be something that you can remember and that becomes part and parcel of who you are.
- The main objective of developing a mission statement is to create one that totally resonates with you. It has to encapsulate your hopes, dreams, and aspirations for the way you want to live your life and the way you want to run your business.
- Your professional mission statement is simply your business road map. It's your calling card and your signature that clarifies why you are in business, what you stand for, and how you help people.
- Clients want to work with people who have clear and deeply held beliefs and convictions. When you've got your mission and vision "right" for you, your passion, commitment, and authenticity will shine through, and clients will be drawn to that.

6

SET SMAC-CERTIFIED GOALS

*"What you get by achieving your goals is not as important
as what you become by achieving your goals."*

—ZIG ZIGLAR

By now, you should be clear about your values, have identified your meaningful purpose, created a compelling vision for your future, and developed a personal and professional mission statement. The last step in the Blueprinting process is to tie all these together by setting goals.

Ideally, each of your goals should dovetail resulting in moving you closer to following your values, fulfilling your meaningful purpose, and living your mission and vision. Goals are the mechanism that delineates what you should be working on day in, day out to get you where you want to go. If you're meeting your short-term goals, that will help you achieve your medium-term goals. If you're meeting your medium-term goals, that will help you achieve your long-term goals. And if you achieve your long-term goals, then God bless you, you've made it.

Goals help you measure progress. In this sense, goals are like a baseball game. The game's not over for nine innings, but along the way you measure your result each inning to see how you're progressing. If you've done the right things for eight innings, chances are good you'll win the game. If you've played lousy for eight innings, you could still win but it's going to take a lucky break. We don't want you to win by getting a lucky break. We want you to win by methodically preparing yourself to win.

Goals are one of the keys to methodically preparing yourself to win.

ESSENTIAL GOAL-SETTING CONCEPTS

Thousands of books have been written about the goal-setting process, but they essentially boil down to a few basic concepts that we're going to share with you. The essential concepts are as follows:

Make your goals SMAC certified. SMAC stands for specific, measurable, achievable, and compatible. One of the biggest reasons why goal setting frequently fails is that the goals do not meet this test. Let's look at each requirement individually:

- *Specific*—your goals have to be clear in terms of the desired outcome. A general goal doesn't cut it. It has to be a discrete goal that can be clearly identified.
- *Measurable*—your goals have to be quantifiable. There must be some way to measure whether the goal has been achieved. For example, "improving your client service" is not a measurable goal. However, if you said "improve my client service by increasing our client satisfaction survey rating from 8.5 to 9.5 by year-end 2006," that would be a good, measurable goal.
- *Achievable*—your goals should have about a 50–50 probability of being achieved. This means you'll have to stretch to achieve them, but they won't be so outlandish that you become demoralized in the process.

- *Compatible*—your goals have to be in harmony with your values, meaningful purpose, and mission. Any incongruity will disrupt your ability to achieve your goals and cause great internal angst.

Think big. We can all do so much more than we think is possible. No doubt you can think of an example of a substantial achievement you've accomplished that at one time may have seemed nearly impossible. When you challenge yourself with a big goal and you connect, accomplishing that goal with a deeply held value, success will not be far behind.

Break big goals into smaller goals and steps. Going from $250,000 in production to $2 million is not going to happen overnight. To accomplish a big goal like this, break it down into smaller goals, such as growing your income by 30 percent a year for eight years. Then set goals to accomplish activities that will help you achieve your yearly goal of 30 percent growth. Accomplishing these smaller steps not only gets you closer to your ultimate goal but also gives you positive reinforcement along the way.

Here's another example of taking a big goal and breaking it down into smaller, more manageable goals and steps. Steve used to work for a broker-dealer, and in mid-1997, the firm set a goal of growing its assets under management from $650 million to $2 billion by the year 2000. To get there, the firm implemented a series of intermediate steps. These intermediate steps included the following:

- Developing additional fee-based programs that would appeal to a broader range of advisors
- Developing a "How to Profit from Managed Accounts" booklet that taught advisors how to make the conversion from commissions to fees and why that was in their best interest

- Aggressively marketing the program to the firm's commission-based advisors
- Developing a monthly educational newsletter for the advisors
- Focusing on recruiting fee-based advisors

All of these intermediate steps helped lead the firm toward its ultimate goal of $2 billion by 2000. By December 1999, the $2 billion target was hit.

You may have a goal of working only Tuesday through Thursday instead of the six days a week you may be working now. Here are five intermediate steps you could take to make that happen:

1. You could systematize your backoffice procedures to make them more efficient so your staff can get more done in less time.
2. You could revamp the way you manage money by setting up model portfolios and a watch list, both of which will significantly reduce the amount of time you spend managing and monitoring assets.
3. You could upgrade your staff so you have only A+ staff members.
4. You could delegate more so that you're doing only the activities that require your expertise and in which you have a strong interest.
5. You could rework your calendar so no appointments are scheduled for Mondays and Fridays.

By breaking the larger goal of working three days a week instead of six into smaller steps, you are in essence developing a plan and timeline to make it happen.

Get your senses involved. As you think about achieving this goal, what does it sound like? What does it feel like? What does it taste like? What does it smell like? Get your whole self involved, which in turn will mobilize your body into taking action and moving forward toward reaching your goal.

Commit your goals to paper. Many people say they have goals, but unfortunately they're "between-the-ears" goals—that is, unwritten goals that only exist in their head. Between-the-ears goals are basically worthless, as Steve explains:

> In the summer of 1980, I visited Puyallup, Washington, just south of Seattle. As the sky cleared one morning, I got my first view of the spectacular, glacier-covered Mount Rainier. Immediately captivated, I turned to my mom and said, "I'm going to come back and climb that someday." Not surprisingly, this "between-the-ears" goal laid dormant for more than 20 years, until a magazine article on mountain climbing triggered my memory in the summer of 2003. This time, I wrote down the goal, superimposed a picture of Mount Rainier in the background, looked at it every morning for the next nine months, and trained hard to get myself in peak physical condition. Sure enough, at 7:05 AM on June 25, 2004, I stood on the summit and raised my ice axe in jubilation, while secretly praying for a helicopter to carry my exhausted body back down the mountain.

Clearly, something magical takes place when you put pencil to paper and commit to your goals. Make sure what you commit to paper you commit to implement. Constantly remind yourself of your goals by keeping them front and center in your life. Ron keeps a copy in his shower and in his briefcase so he's never far away from them.

Believe you can achieve your goals. If you set a goal but don't believe deep down inside that you have a chance of achieving it, then it's not going to happen. Your subconscious mind will be fighting you all the way, and that's a battle you're not going to win.

And not only do you have to believe you can achieve it, you've got to *want* to achieve it. Don't set a goal because it's something you think you should do or because it's something that somebody else wants you to do. Your goals have to be *your* goals and nobody else's expectation of your goals.

Take massive action to get your goal-attainment process started. Setting a goal and writing it down on paper is a great start, but if that's all you do, the goal will never be achieved. You've got to take action. Rather than starting meekly with a baby step, start with a confident, bold action. Do something significant that awakens your body and tells your subconscious mind that things are different this time. Send a message to your subconscious mind you're through monkeying around with half-baked goals that you can easily walk away from.

By taking massive action to get started on your goals, you will set in motion a chain reaction that if kept up—even during times when you're not seeing results—will, like a tsunami, come to fruition with massive force.

GOAL-SETTING EXERCISE

Now what we'd like you to do is take out a piece of paper. Create three columns and label them Professional, Personal, and Fitness. We want you to start putting pencil to paper and get a few ideas for goals you'd like to have. So here's the exercise. For the next 60 seconds, write down as many professional goals you can think of. Don't worry whether the goals make sense; just do a brain dump and get as many goals on paper as you can.

Now do the same thing for personal goals. For 60 seconds, write down as many personal goals as come to mind. And, finally, write down some fitness goals for 60 seconds.

Was that easy? When you're not concerned about overanalyzing your goals, they come out a lot easier. Once you have them all on paper, you can refine them and determine which ones meet the SMAC test and which ones are goals that you'd truly like to achieve. If you ever get stuck during the Blueprinting process, consider doing a timed "brain dump" like this. It just might shake loose the cobwebs and unlock your writer's block.

To complete the goal-setting process, go to Figure 6.1 and review the goal-setting exercise. Figure 6.1 contains a sample goal-setting template that identifies several goals and the key activity needed to complete those goals.

To complete your goals for years three, five, and ten, simply photocopy the Figure 6.2 template. Figure 6.3 contains a Visualize and Realize template that allows you to transfer your one-, three-, five-, and ten-year goals onto one page so you can see how they link together to allow you to move closer to your compelling vision of the future.

FIGURE 6.1 *Sample Year 1 Goals and Action Plan*

GOAL	Key Activity to Achieve
5 new A+ clients	Implement coaching program
One major family vacation	Schedule it
Vigorous activity at least 4 days per week	Get up by 5:15
Break 90 in golf	Eliminate double and triple bogies
Complete 15 hours of C.E.	Attend FPA meetings
Close office at noon on Friday during the summer	Communicate the change to clients
Spend 5 hours/week helping kids with homework	Make it a priority

FIGURE 6.2 *Goals and Action Plan*

Year ____ Your Age ____ Spouse ____ Kids ____	
GOAL	**Key Activity to Achieve**

FIGURE 6.3 *Visualize and Realize*

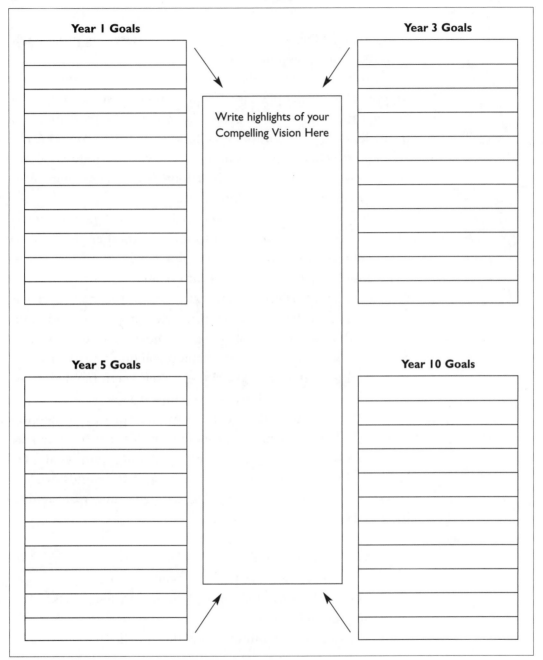

ADDITIONAL THOUGHTS ON GOAL SETTING

Here are a few other thoughts on the goal-setting process that we'd like you to keep in mind.

First, improve the odds of meeting your goals by enlisting the support of other people. Find people you know will be supportive and tell them about your goals. These could be your spouse, a dear friend, or even a business colleague. By telling someone else about your goals, that person now has a vested interest too and could become instrumental in helping you reach them. Also, sharing your goals puts a little more pressure on you to reach them. If nobody knew about your goals and you failed to achieve them, you'd only have to answer to yourself. If other people know about your goals and you fail, it's a little harder to take.

Second, as you embark on your goal-setting process, lighten your load. Think about all the extra "stuff" you have either at home or in the office. Do some spring-cleaning and get rid of the stuff you don't need. If your office is a mess, clean it up. Get rid of papers, files, magazines, and trinkets you don't need anymore. By shedding dead weight, you'll feel better. You'll feel lighter on your feet, and you'll feel like moving forward.

Third, systematize your goal achievement process by developing rituals. Start implementing some activities that become positive habits and move you closer to reaching your goals. For example, let's say one of your goals is to lose 15 pounds by a certain date. To aid you in reaching this goal, you could create a morning ritual similar to the following:

1. Get out of bed at 5:30.
2. Start drinking a one-half liter bottle of water.
3. Get on the treadmill for a 10-minute warm-up walk.
4. Jog for 30 minutes.
5. Finish with a 10-minute warm-down walk.

6. Take a shower.
7. Eat a healthy breakfast with your family that includes egg whites and a fruit smoothie with flax seeds.

Following a ritual similar to this would be a great way to start your day. You get your blood pumping; you get your body filled with great nutrients; and you spend some quality time with your family. By the time you jump into the car to go to your office, you're feeling great and ready to embrace all the day's opportunities.

Fourth, identify the 5 percent of your activities that generate 50 percent of your results and concentrate on them. We've all heard of the 80/20 rule, but there's a modification to that rule that suggests 5 percent of our activities account for 50 percent of our results. Figure out what those key activities are for you, develop goals to spend more time engaged in those activities, and you'll see your results soar.

And fifth, maintain a balance between victory and sacrifice. Achieving your goals is important but don't lose sight of what really matters as Pahom found out in Leo Tolstoy's 1886 short story "How Much Land Does a Man Need."

In this insightful story, Pahom, an ambitious Russian peasant, was presented with an irresistible opportunity by the Bashkir tribesmen. For 1,000 rubles, the Bashkir tribesmen offered to sell Pahom as much land as he could walk around in a day. The only stipulation was that Pahom had to start and finish in the same spot and he had to complete his walk by sunset.

With big dollar signs in his eyes, an elated Pahom took off, marked his trail along the way and by afternoon had traveled a great distance. The land was so attractive that it seemed that each time he made a turn, he found a new piece of land that looked appealing, so he kept moving forward and adding to his land. As the day wore on and the sun began to set in the western sky, Pahom realized he better pick up the pace or else he wouldn't make it back to the starting point in time to collect his prize. Perhaps he had gone too far he thought to himself.

As the sun started to drop below the horizon, Pahom began to panic. He was tired and starting to breathe heavily. Despite his exhaustion, he told himself he couldn't stop now or else everybody would call him a fool for stopping so close to the finish. So with every ounce of energy, he put one leg in front of the other and hurled his body forward. Finally, he lunged at the finish line and touched the spot just as the sun set.

He made it . . . or did he? Pahom was so exhausted that he could not get up and died on the spot.

As the story ends, Pahom's servant picked up a spade and dug his grave. Turns out that all the land Pahom needed was just 6 feet long by 3 feet wide.

Goals are great but always keep them in perspective.

SUMMARY

- Ideally, each of your goals should dovetail with moving you closer to following your values, fulfilling your meaningful purpose, and living your mission and vision. Goals are the mechanisms that delineate what you should be working on day in, day out to get you where you want to go.
- Make your goals specific, measurable, achievable, and compatible.
- Commit your goals to paper.
- Take massive action to get your goal-attainment process started.
- Improve the odds of meeting your goals by enlisting the support of other people.
- As you embark on your goal-setting process, lighten your load. Do some spring-cleaning and get rid of the "stuff" you don't need both at home and at the office.

- Systematize your goal achievement process by developing rituals. Start implementing some activities that become positive habits and move you closer to reaching your goals.

TNT #1 ACTION STEPS

- Complete the five Blueprinting exercises. You may be tempted to skip them or go no deeper with them than surface level, but don't make that mistake. Take your time, dig deep, and develop your personal blueprint for success.

- Identify your values and consciously live them day in, day out.

- Find your meaningful purpose in life and fully embrace it.

- Create a compelling vision for your future, draw energy from it, and move toward it in your daily activities.

- Develop a personal and professional mission statement to keep you on track in your business and in your life.

- Set SMAC-certified goals (specific, measurable, achievable, compatible) that measure your progress toward fulfilling your mission and moving you toward your compelling vision.

- Download and complete the Vision/Mission/Goals template from the Peak Productions Web site at http://www.peakproductions.com. Print the template in color, take it to a local printer, get two copies laminated, and keep one at home where you'll see it every day and one with you at the office.

- Review your vision, mission, and goals on a daily basis.

GET THE RIGHT PEOPLE ON THE TEAM

7

PUT MORE SCIENCE INTO THE ART OF HIRING AND COMPENSATING STAFF

"No person will make a great business who wants to do it all himself or get all the credit."
—ANDREW CARNEGIE

Early in life we learned that 1 + 1 = 2. In business we learned about synergy where 1 + 1 can equal 3. Top achievers use a different math. They transform 1 + 1 into 1 next to 1 and come up with 11. That's the value of an A+ team that's operating at peak performance.

One of the key hurdles for many advisors is hiring and compensating qualified staff. Clearly it's an issue that prevents many advisors from ever reaching breakthrough production levels and from ever having a healthy and fulfilling quality of life. Although there are no easy answers, you can take certain steps and put systems in place to make sure you employ a quality staff that works in concert with you to move your business forward.

As TNT #2, staffing issues have to be addressed early and your A+ staff has to be in place before you can take your business and your life to the next level. We'll begin by addressing when to hire a new staff person. From there we'll discuss compensating your staff, and then we'll finish with a detailed discussion of our five-step process for hiring a quality staff.

Never forget that if you want to attract and retain A+ and A clients and have a great quality of life, you have to have A+-level and A-level staff members.

WHEN TO HIRE A NEW STAFF MEMBER

We're going to put you to work now and ask you to do a couple of exercises. First, pull out your calculator, take your annual gross commissions and fee income, and divide that number by 1,840. The result is your average hourly income based on working 40 hours per week for 46 weeks out of the year. Second, pull out a piece of paper and for the next few minutes make a list of all the activities you do during a typical week. Now, go back over your list and put a check mark by any activity that you could theoretically hire somebody to do for you for less than the average hourly wage you calculated in step one.

Do you have a lot of check marks? If so, you're infected with the "dollar time, penny work" disease. This simply means you're using your time to do things that you could hire someone else to do at a much lower cost and probably with a far better result. It's like having a farm in the middle of downtown. The land is not being utilized for its highest and best use. Spending your time on $10-an-hour work is no different.

Up to this point, you may have rationalized this work situation by saying:

1. I don't have enough revenue-producing activities to keep me busy full-time, so it's cheaper for me to do some of this work myself instead of hiring someone to do it for me;
2. I'm the only one who can do these activities, because there's a certain way I like to do it and no one else can do it this way;
3. I can't afford to hire another staff person;

4. It's easier for me to do it than to explain how to do it to someone else.

Of course, you can rationalize all you want but if you really want to achieve breakthrough performance, you've got to stop rationalizing and start mobilizing. One of the quickest ways you can grow your business is to hire a staff person to do your busy work which will free you up to work on your highest value activities.

Our philosophy is to hire staff people to do all the work for you that can be done for less than your average hourly wage. If you average $200 per hour, it doesn't make sense to spend your time on $20 per hour work. The same is true for your Team Leaders. If they're making $25 an hour, they shouldn't spend their time on $10 an hour work. You might argue that your Team Leader has enough time to do the $10 an hour work so why not have him or her do it and save the expense of hiring another person? Well consider this. How powerful would it be if your Team Leader, instead of spending 12 hours per week on $10 an hour work, spent those 12 hours calling your A+ and A clients? How powerful would it be if your Team Leader spent those 12 hours performing random acts of kindness for your A+ and A clients?

The point is, by spending your time on your highest and best use activities, you'll earn much more money than you'll save by doing the penny work yourself.

COMPENSATING YOUR STAFF

One of the most common questions we receive is, how much should I pay my staff? It's a critical question because compensation is an important factor in job performance. The "right" compensation plan can help you get extra effort from your staff and make your firm more productive and profitable. The "wrong" compensation plan can put you out of business.

The old saying, "You get what you pay for," is true when it comes to staffing. We've learned the hard way that hiring someone at a "bargain" rate brings you "bargain bin" results. We've always received the most value when we hired the best people possible and paid them accordingly. Think of your staff not as an expense but as an investment. Done well, your staff will be one of the best investments you ever make.

What do you call the gap between an employee doing just enough to keep their job and an employee operating at 100 percent of their ability? Ron calls this gap "discretionary effort." It's the amount of effort that is lying dormant in your organization and, if awakened, could propel your firm to stellar success.

You know what we're talking about here. You probably have people on staff who are going through the motions and doing just enough to get by. They're not so bad that you would fire them, but they're not setting the world on fire either. Perhaps your clients love them. Perhaps you're thinking it's just easier to keep them on staff than it is to go through the hassle of finding and training a new employee who may or may not work out. Rationalizations are easy. The hard part is doing what you know is the right thing to do.

Consider this. Let's say your "just enough to get by" staff member was put into a life or death situation. How much effort and energy do you think that person would expend trying to survive? Undoubtedly, he or she would summon a Herculean effort to survive and would discover being capable of far more than he or she ever thought possible.

Fortunately, compensating a staff member is not a life-or-death situation. But you can structure a compensation system that will get life-or-death results from them.

After years of fiddling with various compensation plans, Ron developed a compensation system that he calls *results-based pay*. It's really a broad-based pay structure that incorporates several goals. First, it ties every staff member into the firm's overall performance and encourages team effort; staff members have a vested interest in the success of the firm. Second, it rewards individuals for adding value. Even though we want a strong team, we also want strong individuals because not all our work involves team effort. Third, it's flexible. The staff is compensated with the things it values, whether more pay, more time off, or both.

As Ron is fond of saying, "What gets measured gets done," and results-based pay is all about developing measurements and getting things done.

Here's how it works. Each staff member receives a base salary that is commensurate with his or her experience and with going market rates. Each is then eligible for a bonus based 60 percent on meeting individual goals and 40 percent on meeting team goals. The bonus is paid quarterly and can be paid in the form of cash, time off, or a combination of both. Conceptually, it's very simple. Here are some of the details.

Our base salaries are targeted near the 50th percentile for that position in our market. How do you know what the 50th percentile salary is for your position? We recommend you check out the http://www.salary.com Web site. At this site, you can look up the 50th percentile salary for just about any position imaginable and can tailor the results to your specific geographic location.

For example, let's say you are hiring a receptionist (Director of First Impression at our firm) in Omaha. According to http://www.salary.com, the 50th percentile salary for a receptionist in Omaha in July 2004 was $24,110. In addition, the site tells us the average bonus for a receptionist is $290, which brings the total compensation to $24,400. By contrast, the site tells us the 75th percentile salary for this position is $26,969 and with bonus is $27,470. Armed with this information, you could confidently make a base salary offer in the low- to mid-20s and know you are in the ballpark—but that's only part of the story.

On top of the base salary, we have to add the bonus. As mentioned above, the bonus is based 60 percent on meeting individual goals and 40 percent on meeting team goals.

Individual Goals (60 percent of total bonus)

These goals can be whatever is appropriate for a specific position in your office but make sure they meet the SMAC test (Specific, Measurable, Achievable, Compatible). Also, make sure the goals are designed to help you further *your* goals. In other words, if your staff members reach their goals, that should directly tie into your reaching your goals for the firm.

Team Goals (40 percent of total bonus)

These are goals that you'd like to accomplish as a firm and are not directly tied to any one person at your firm. For example, below are six of Carson Wealth Management Group's team goals from previous years, although your goals may differ based on the particular needs of your practice:

1. Twenty-four creative ideas that add material value (6 per quarter)
2. Eighty random acts of kindness (20 per quarter)
3. Contact A+ clients monthly and A and B clients quarterly
4. Five percent reduction in office expenses versus prior year
5. Twenty-four referrals (6 per quarter)
6. Maintain client satisfaction index rating of 10 or higher.

The team goal bonus of 40 percent is broken into two parts. Half of this bonus is tied into achieving the client satisfaction index rating of a 10 or higher goal. The other half of the 40 percent is based on meeting 80 percent of the team goals. For example, if you have five team goals, then meeting 80 percent of those goals would require achieving four of them. If your team met at least four of the five goals, then the team would be eligible for the other half of its 40 percent bonus.

Effectively, the team has to hit at least 80 percent of the team goals or else its payout is low.

So how much should your bonus be? We believe it should be a percentage of the staff member's base pay and should range somewhere between 25 to 40 percent of the base pay. For example, let's use our receptionist example from above and assume the base pay is $23,000. The annual bonus (to be paid in quarterly installments) for this position would range between $5,750 and $9,200. For someone making $23,000 a year, that's a nice bonus and a good incentive to make a discretionary effort. Notice the base pay plus the bonus puts the receptionist's total compensation above the 75th percentile as identified on http://www.salary.com.

The extra output that you'll get from the discretionary effort bonus of $5,750 to $9,200 is equivalent to the output of one staff person. The beauty of it is you don't have the cost of furnishing the person a computer, work space, and all the other costs associated with an additional staff person.

Our philosophy is to pay above-market rates for great performers. Paying 25 percent above the market rate for a great performer is a bargain compared with what that person can generate in return. Of course, this works only for great performers. Paying 25 percent above the market rate for an average performer is charity, and you're not in a charity business.

You could also let the staff member substitute time off for giving up some cash bonus. As a caveat, don't let the additional time off exceed one week or else you may put too much of strain on the rest of your staff.

So far we've talked about monetary compensation and paid time off. What about other benefits?

To attract top-notch employees, you'll need to offer a well-rounded compensation package. At a minimum, we recommend you offer a retirement plan and a medical plan. Your retirement plan should offer some type of matching benefit. The average matching benefit for U.S. companies is about 3 percent, so if you stay in that range, you should be fine. For example, if you offer a 401(k) plan, you could match $.50 out of each $1.00 employees contribute up to the first 6 percent of their contribution.

In the medical benefits area, you should offer a group plan or offer a financial allowance that employees can use to buy insurance on their own. Either way, at a minimum your benefit should be equal to the annual premium for employees. If the employees choose coverage for more than just themselves, they would pay the difference between the coverage they chose and the individual employee rate.

As you well know, employee benefits are not cheap, but staff members don't always appreciate how much extra you invest in them through the benefits package. That's why we share with our staff members the cost (investment) of benefits. We show them the value of their paid time off, their salary, their 401(k) match, their health insurance, and the FICA benefit paid by the company. It lets the staff know that the amount of money we invest in them goes well beyond the base pay and bonus.

What we've just described is a minimum benefits package. You could offer more depending on your financial situation and how you want to position your business. For example, we've implemented what we call our "Above and Beyond" Program. At the beginning of each year, all staff members receive six Above and Beyond certificates that they can award to another staff member for service that goes Above and Beyond the call of duty. The recipient of the certificate can turn it in for one hour's worth of time off. In addition, at the end of the year, the staff member with the most Above and Beyond certificates gets an extra award that could be time off, a trip, or something else of significant value. This works well in larger offices and is a great way to build camaraderie.

THE FIVE-STEP PROCESS FOR HIRING QUALIFIED STAFF

Jim Collins, author of the best-selling book *Good to Great,* discovered that one of the key traits of companies that went from being good to great was their focus on the people. Specifically, these companies "got the right people on the bus, the wrong people off the bus, and the right people in the right seat." The five steps to hiring an A+ staff are these:

1. Evaluate your current staffing situation.
2. Develop detailed job descriptions.
3. Search for candidates.
4. Screen and interview candidates.
5. Make the offer.

Step #1. Evaluate Your Current Staffing Situation

The first step in the hiring process is to evaluate your current staffing situation. Do you have too many staff members? Do you have too few? Do you have the right staff members? This third question is the real key. You've got to make sure you have the right staff members and then you can adjust and build from there.

Reviewing your staff members individually to determine if they are the right team members for you, simply rate each team member as either an A+, A, B, C, or D employee.

A+ staff members are, of course, what you're striving for. These are employees who have great personalities, outstanding work habits, and get the job done no matter what it takes. Like A+ clients, these are the staff members you want to clone.

A staff members are your bread-and-butter employees. Not quite as good as A+ employees, but they're definitely keepers and can help you get where you want to go. With a little more training and direction, they may even be able to move up to the A+ level.

B employees are good people, but they just don't have the extra oomph you need, or their job may not be designed to take full advantage of their skills, knowledge, interests, and abilities. They do their job as required but don't make the extra effort to go above and beyond. With proper training, direction, and perhaps a shifting of responsibilities, B-level employees may be able to move up to A-level within 90 days.

C-level staffers are similar to B staffers except it's clear they're never going to move up a level.

D-level employees are obvious; they shouldn't be on your payroll.

Here's the hard part. D- and C-level employees have to be let go immediately. B employees are on the bubble. Work with them to determine what you can do to move them up to A level. Take no more than 90 days, and if they are able to move up a level, great; if not, they have to go too. It may sound cruel but it's really not. Frequently, when an employee is not performing well, it's because that employee is in the wrong job. By letting the person go, you may actually be doing him or her a favor by forcing that employee to find a new opportunity that's a better fit. We've seen this happen on numerous occasions.

Concurrent with your staff evaluation, we want you to develop two organization charts. The first one should depict your current situation and the second one should depict your ideal future organization. There may be a big gap between the two and that's okay.

As a small business owner, you have to wear a lot of different hats. Consequently, your current organization chart may have your name in most of the boxes. But as you build your practice, we want you to put the people in place, the systems in place, and the organization in place so that you end up just focusing on those two or three or four things that you are really, really good at and that you really enjoy. Your future organization chart will depict your ultimate staffing structure. Some advisors want a big staff whereas others are content with just two or three. Either way's fine; you just need to know what the number is for you because that will help determine how many clients you can handle and how much revenue you can generate.

Here's a good rule of thumb: When you've completely systematized your practice and up-scaled your client list, you should be able to generate about $350,000 to $400,000 in gross revenue per staff person. How close are you to that today?

With the above rule of thumb in mind, we've developed a staffing model that is based on building a $2.0 million to $2.5 million practice. It calls for five staff members plus yourself. See Figure 7.1. Here are brief descriptions of the five staff members in the order they should be hired.

FIGURE 7.1 *Where Do I Start?*

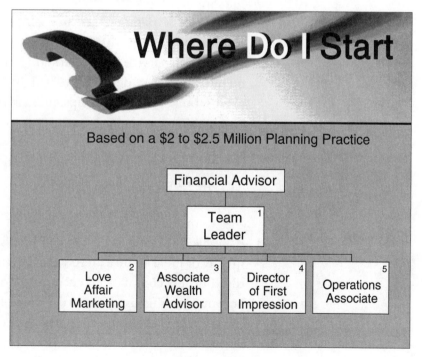

1. *Team Leader.* In the beginning, it's you and your Team
   Leader. In essence, the Team Leader wears numerous hats
   and does all the stuff that you don't want to do. The Team
   Leader should be a highly talented, fully licensed person
   who has the ability to grow as your business grows. Among
   other things, he or she is responsible for ensuring the ef-
   fective implementation and use of your internal systems.
   Eventually, the Team Leader will be a key part of your or-
   ganization and will take a huge load off your back. Key job
   activities include:
   - Administrative
   - Compliance
   - Operations
   - Trading
   - Maintaining systems manual
   - Coordinating team meetings
   - Supervising staff

2. *Love Affair Marketing.* Once you get your systems in place,
   you can hire a Love Affair Marketing person to ramp up
   your client service and marketing activities. This staff
   member will get deeply involved in working with your
   clients, building relationships, making proactive outbound
   touch-base calls, making birthday calls, and setting up client events. Key job activities include:
   - Making proactive, outbound relationship calls
   - Coordinating client events
   - Marketing
   - Coordinating client newsletter

3. *Associate Wealth Advisor.* One of the keys to improving your
   quality of life is to hire an Associate Wealth Advisor to handle your less complicated accounts. Moving some of these
   accounts to this associate frees you to spend more time
   pursuing and working with higher net worth clients. You'll
   also have more time to deepen the relationship with those

clients who are most important to you. Key activities of this advisor include the following:

- Handling your less complicated accounts
- Developing new accounts of his or her own
- Assisting in investment research
- Assisting you as requested

4. *Director of First Impression.* More than just a receptionist, your Director of First Impression is an outstanding people person who sets the tone and creates a pleasant and comfortable environment for your clients and prospects when they step through your door. Key activities of this director include the following:

- Answering the phone
- Greeting clients and prospects
- Sorting and distributing mail
- Handling office supplies
- Coordinating with vendors
- Scheduling

5. *Operations Associate.* As your business grows, you'll need to add a second operations person who can relieve your Team Leader of certain duties and allow your Team Leader to perform more supervisory functions. This person should also be heavily cross-trained and function as an all-around pinch hitter in the office. Key activities include the following:

- General operations, new accounts, transfers
- Coordinating advisor licensing
- Preparing client updates and reviews

Getting your organization to look like this is an evolutionary process. Start by hiring the Team Leader and progress from there. In the beginning, everybody will wear numerous hats, but as your staff grows, you can get more specialized.

The Associate Wealth Advisor position is frequently one of the most difficult to fill. You need a candidate who is polished and poised, aggressive yet not overbearing, internally motivated, service oriented, and willing to work under your guidance. Typically, this would be someone with a couple of years of industry experience who is looking for a smaller office environment with an opportunity to work alongside an experienced advisor. To find this candidate, get the word out to your industry colleagues. Contact the local FPA chapter to see if members have a way to promote your job opening. You could even try posting the position on http://www.monster.com. Some advisors have had success converting one of their existing staff members to an Associate Wealth Advisor so don't overlook that possibility.

How should you compensate the Associate Wealth Advisor? We recommend a 35 percent payout, but that can vary depending on the services you provide. Figure 7.2 can be used as a guide for what you should be paid for the various services you provide.

To get your Associate Wealth Advisor started, consider paying a salary of $25,000 to $35,000 the first year (depending on experience). In return for the salary, you should keep 100 percent of

FIGURE 7.2 *Compensation Guide for Services Provided*

Services You Provide	Override Required
Supervision	15%
Office Space	10%
Phone/Computer Software	5%
Leads	5%
Office Staff Support	8%
Co-op Programs	
(Love Affair Marketing, holiday brunch, client events, etc.)	5%
Health Insurance	5%
401(k)	5%
Sales Training	4%
Marketing Material/Seminars	3%

any commissions or fees that are generated. In year two, they would become independent contractors, their salary would go away, and they would be compensated solely on commissions and fees. All accounts should be set up as joint accounts with you.

There are three objectives when hiring an Associate Wealth Advisor. First, it will free up your time so you can devote more effort to your top clients and prospects. Accordingly, over the course of the first year, gradually move some of your less complicated accounts to the new advisor. You may have to do some joint meetings initially to smooth this over with your clients, but most will be okay with it. Tell your clients that they're not losing you, they're simply getting a new person to meet with but you still review all accounts and you work closely with the new advisor. Your Associate Wealth Advisor should eventually handle all your B and C clients. You should handle the A+ and A clients; the D clients should be fired (we'll discuss client profiling in detail a little later).

The second objective when hiring an Associate Wealth Advisor is to allow you to more quickly increase your account minimum. Setting an account minimum and sticking to it is a simple yet very effective way to increase your income. Remember, you won't double your income by doubling the number of clients you have. You'll double your income by increasing the net worth of the clients you have. Anybody who comes through your door with investable assets less than your minimum can now be handled by your Associate Wealth Advisor.

And third, an effective Associate Wealth Advisor will have a positive impact on your quality of life. You should be able to leave the office and not have to worry about trades being placed or clients' questions being answered. Plus, with fewer clients to deal with, you'll have more time to do the things you enjoy and more time to spend with the clients you like.

Step #2. Develop Detailed Job Descriptions

The second step is to put together a detailed job description. Writing a job description forces you to organize your thoughts about exactly what you want the person in that position to do. Not only is that a good idea for you but it's also great for the candidate. With a written job description, the candidate will have a better idea of what the job entails and can make a more informed decision whether joining your firm is a good fit.

Four basic parts make up a job description. The first part is just a description of what the actual job is and doesn't have to be in great detail. It's a high-level overview of the position and how it fits into the overall organization.

The second part outlines the responsibilities and the activities for the position. Go into some detail here so the candidates know pretty clearly what they will be working on. You may even want to put a percentage next to the major items to show what percent of their time may be spent in each area. Now, granted in an advisory practice, things will come up that are not covered in the responsibilities and activities section and that's fine. Just make candidates aware that the job description covers the main activities, and there may be other activities that are required too.

The third part of a job description identifies your expectations for the position. This is where you need to put some of your individuality into the description. As an entrepreneur, you have certain ways of doing business and certain standards of conduct that you want your employees to live up to. This is the section where you can list those. It allows your firm's culture to shine through. For example, if your office opens at 8:00 in the morning, you may expect everybody to arrive before 8:00, get their coffee and chitchat out of the way, fire up their computers, and be productively working by 8:00 versus arriving at 8:00 and not becoming productive until 8:10. You're unique; let that show in your expectations.

The fourth part of the job description identifies the knowledge, skills, and abilities that candidates are going to need to be successful in the position. You want to make it clear what the requirements are for the job for candidates to be successful in the job. For example, they may need to have a securities license, a certain level of expertise, a great attitude, outstanding interpersonal skills, and excellent customer service skills. In a moment, we'll show you an example of how you can test your candidates to identify what type of customer service skills they may have.

If you can put this job description together in advance, it will really help you clarify the type of candidate that you need so that as you go through the interview process, you'll be able to pick up on these things and be able to make a better hiring decision.

Figure 7.3 is an example of a job description for the Team Leader.

FIGURE 7.3 *Job Description for the Team Leader*

Description:
The Team Leader plays a crucial role in the smooth functioning of the office. With overall responsibility for the office, the Team Leader must be able to work effectively with other staff members, clients, and the Wealth Advisor(s).

Responsibilities and Activities:
- Handles compliance issues
  - Maintains compliance manual
  - Oversees audits
  - Obtains advertising approval
- Handles trading issues
  - Placing trades, rebalancing accounts
  - Reviewing confirms
  - Sending prospectuses and switch letters
- Handles training and continuing education
- Handles new business
  - Meets with clients and starts new client forms processing
  - Follows up with clients as needed to make sure all paperwork is processed

(continued)

FIGURE 7.3 *Job Description for the Team Leader, continued*

Responsibilities and Activities, continued:
- Handles commission processing
  - Reviews commission statements to ensure accuracy
- Coordinates daily team meeting
  - Sets agenda
  - Disseminates minutes, resulting tasks, and timelines for completion
- Supervises staff (except Associate Wealth Advisor)
  - Hiring and training
  - Performance reviews
  - General supervision
- Develops and maintains written systems of all activities of the staff
- Writes down the six most important activities and prioritizes them each day before leaving office

Expectations:
- At his or her desk, productively working by 8:00 AM
- Has the six most important activities list on his or her desk before leaving each evening
- Does not eat lunch at the desk
- Phone calls received by 3:00 in the afternoon are returned the same day. Phone calls received after 3:00 are returned the next morning.
- Changes voice mail greeting each day to reflect the date and whether in or out of the office and, if out, when the caller can expect a return call
- Works weekends or evenings as necessitated by client events

Knowledge, Skills, and Abilities:
- Requires:
  - Excellent knowledge of the securities industry's rules and regulations
  - Knowledge of NASD Series 7, 24, 63 (and 65 if needed for your Registered Investment Advisor)
  - Excellent analytical skills
  - Excellent interpersonal skills
  - Excellent organizational and time management skills
  - Excellent attitude and an extraordinary client service orientation
  - Ability to handle multiple tasks and operate on tight deadlines
- Helpful:
  - Previous supervisory experience

You can share the job description with your candidates during the interview process, but there's a specific time during the interview process that we'd prefer you share it, and we'll get to that in a moment. A well-written job description helps ensure that you hire people who have a clear understanding of what the job entails. This reduces staff turnover by eliminating those people who quit early on and say, "The job is not what I expected."

Step #3. Search for Candidates

The third step is to search for candidates. We frequently are asked, "Where can I find good candidates?" The answer: be creative. Here are a few of the ways we've found good candidates over the years.

First, get the word out that you're looking for a new staff member and ask for a referral. Just as we try to build our advisory practice through referrals from A + clients, we can get the word out to our friends, business colleagues, clients, and other associates to let them know we're looking for a new staff member. There is, however, a potential downside to this approach that you should keep in mind. If you get a referral but decide not to hire the person, is that going to hurt the relationship with the person who gave you the referral? It shouldn't, but just keep that in mind and make sure you circle back with the person who gave you the referral and let him or her know the status.

Second, go online. Web sites such as http://www.monster.com and http://www.hotjobs.com can be a cost-effective place to find qualified candidates. Also, look at your local newspaper, which probably has an online section where you can post your position. We suggest that you omit your address in the ad and require candidates to attach their résumé and a cover letter and respond via e-mail. This takes advantage of one of the side benefits of an online service—you know the person responding has some computer and

Internet skills. That's important because most of our jobs are going to require computer skills to some degree. Requiring a cover letter is very helpful too because it forces candidates to write a letter and tell you more about themselves. It also helps you gauge their writing skills and their persuasion skills.

Third, check universities and educational institutions. There are approximately 300 CFP Board-Registered programs at more than 180 colleges and universities nationwide that are training people to become Certified Financial Planners (CFPs). If you're looking for an associate advisor, this could be a good place to check. To find an institution near you, go to http://www.cfp.net and click on "Become a CFP Professional." The Web site allows you to search by state and by educational program type. When you find a match, get on the phone and call the institution's placement office and let it know you've got a position available. Ask if you can talk to a professor who's teaching some of these classes. When you get a professor on the phone (or perhaps e-mail), ask who some of the top students are. If you're not near a CFP Board-Registered institution, check your nearest college or university and follow the same strategy. Talk to the placement office and let it know you have a position available. Call some of the professors in the business school and ask who the top students are.

Fourth, consider hiring an intern. If your budget is tight and you can't afford a full-time staff person, go with an intern from the local college or university. Schools love to offer internships to their students, so you should have no trouble filling your position this way. The downside is that the position is temporary and the candidate may not take it as seriously as you'd like. On the other hand, if the intern works out well, he or she may be a candidate to hire full-time after graduation.

Fifth, as you're out and about in the community, keep your eyes and ears open for people with whom you come in contact who appear to have the characteristics you are looking for. Steve used this quite effectively when he went shopping for a new car in the summer of 2003. He was so pleased with the salesperson's service, personality, and interpersonal skills that he asked the salesperson if he were open to learning about a job opportunity. The salesperson said yes and several interviews later, he was hired as a salesperson at Peak Productions. You may run into someone at a department store or a restaurant or anywhere. The point is, stay alert to people who provide great service and have pleasant personalities. They could be your next new hire.

Be creative and persistent in your job search, and it will pay off.

Step #4. Screen and Interview Candidates

The fourth step is to screen and interview the candidates. Your initial screening tool is, of course, the résumé. If you've done a good job up to this point, you should have a stack of résumés to review. As you review them, here are a few things to keep in mind.

First, judge each résumé on composition and professionalism. Which résumés knocked you over with a positive first impression? Which looked as though they were scribbled on the back of a napkin with coffee stains? Which were laid out well and pleasing to the eye? Which ones showed some creativity?

Second, get out your eagle eyes and check the spelling. If there's a misspelling, that's a huge red flag. If candidates didn't pay attention to detail on a document as important as a résumé, then just imagine what they'll do when they're working for you!

Third, determine which résumés are applicable to the position you have available. Sometimes when we place an ad, we get résumés from people who clearly are shopping their application and CV to every employer that has a position available; those are quickly deleted. Other applications come in with a custom cover letter, making it clear these applicants took some time to review the position and have a high level of interest.

Fourth, look for any gaps in applicants' employment. Frequently, we receive résumés that just list the years of employment. For example, they may look like this:

1996–1999   ABC Brokerage Firm . . .
1999–2001   XYZ Brokerage Firm . . .

That's usually a sign that there's a gap in employment. You'll definitely want to ask about that during the interview process and be specific about it. Ask the applicant if he or she were unemployed for a period and, if so, why? Being unemployed for a period is not necessarily a bad thing; you just need to understand why and determine if the reason is a valid one.

Fifth, review the résumé for employment stability. In the past, employees used to stay with one company for years. Today, we see much more job-hopping and less company loyalty. Some job-hopping is legitimate because the work environment has changed. For competitive reasons, companies are quicker to downsize and are less paternalistic. So job-hopping is not so big a red flag as it used to be. However, if you find a candidate who's had five jobs in the past six or seven years, that's an area that needs to be explored during the interview. You'll need to find out exactly why the candidate left each one of those jobs. You'll also have to figure out during an interview if candidates job-hopped because they are clueless about what they want to do with their life. If they're clueless when you hire them, your cost of educating them will be very high.

Interviewing. As you review the résumés, try to pick out five to ten that appear to indicate good candidates for you. In the past, we used to bring this initial group of people in for a live interview. But what we found was that somebody could appear to be absolutely terrific on paper but was a total dud when we saw the candidate in the office. We had wasted our time and the candidate's time.

We've solved this problem by conducting a phone interview for the first screen.

Conducting the initial interview via the phone is a huge time-saver. In a ten-minute phone interview, you can quickly weed out those who do not merit an in-house interview. For example, we recently received a résumé from a candidate who appeared to have everything we were looking for. In the past, we would have immediately contacted the person and set up an in-house interview. But this time we set up a phone interview, and it was a good thing we did. We asked a few questions, and the responses were uninspiring, unoriginal, and unenthusiastic. Then we asked the candidate one final question, "What would your ideal workday look like?" For the next 15 seconds there was so much silence you could have heard an ant crawling on the floor. After the candidate collected his thoughts, he said something very profound: "I really don't know." Clearly, this person had no clue what he wanted to do, and we certainly weren't going to educate him on our nickel.

A phone interview also helps determine candidates' phone skills. Most of the positions in your firm will require some phone time, so determining phone skills early on can save you time later. You also want to hire articulate, enthusiastic people, and the phone helps you identify them.

Here are a couple of phone interviewing strategies that should help you get the most from your calls.

First, schedule your phone interviews one right after another. For example, if you have seven phone interviews, try to schedule them all in the same morning or same afternoon. This allows you to compare each candidate while your thoughts about them are still fresh in your mind. Each call should last no more than about ten minutes.

Second, ask each candidate the same questions. Develop a list of five to seven questions and print them on a sheet of paper with enough space between each question to write notes. During the interview, jot down your notes on the sheet of paper. After the call, do a "brain dump" and write down all the thoughts you can think of about the candidate. When you've finished that, make a determination right then if you want to bring the person in for an in-house interview. Write down your answer on the top of the paper. For those you do not intend to bring in, ask your assistant to send a polite turndown letter.

Here are seven sample questions you may want to ask during the phone interview:

1. *Question:* I have your résumé in front of me, but I'd like you to walk me through it, and tell me about your work experience and your education, so I can get a better feel for your knowledge, skills, and abilities.
   Comment: This question is an easy one for them to answer so it puts them at ease. It also gives you a quick indication of their communication skills and their ability to string together coherent sentences.

2. *Question:* What motivates you?
   Comment: Are they motivated by money? By helping other people? Serving clients? Solving problems? Setting a goal and accomplishing it? The key is you're looking for people who are motivated and have a burning desire to succeed.

3. *Question:* How do you define success?
   Comment: If they say money, skip them; they're too shallow. Their definition of success gets to the heart of their values. Are they compatible with yours?

4. *Question:* What are your long-term goals?
   Comment: This is a standard interview question, so they should be well prepared for it. Be sure their long-term goals are compatible with the opportunities you offer. If not, then you run the risk that they would leave your firm after a short time.

5. *Question:* What achievements are you most proud of and why?

Comment: This gives them an opportunity to brag a little. It also helps you understand how aggressive and competitive they are. If their proudest accomplishments impress you, that's a good sign. You may have some candidates who answer this by discussing personal achievements, such as raising two good kids as a single mom. That's great because it helps you further understand their value system, but also try to elicit a professional achievement.

6. *Question:* What don't you like about your current (or most recent) job?

   Comment: Carefully consider their answer. Does your position entail the same activity or circumstance that a candidate doesn't like?

7. *Question:* What prompted you to apply for this position?

   Comment: Here's their opportunity to sell you on why they are excited about the job and why they think they're a good fit. You also may discover how much research they've done about your firm. For example, if you have a Web site and they mention that they've visited it, that's a good sign.

During the course of the phone interview, a candidate's responses may prompt you to ask another question that's not on this list and that's okay. Just don't let the interview run more than about ten minutes.

There are a couple of ways to end the phone interview.

First, if you are sure you do not want to invite a candidate to an in-house interview, then end the call by saying this:

We're doing phone interviews with a number of candidates, and from that list we'll make a determination of whom we want to invite to come in for an in-house interview. We expect to make that decision by (pick a date but no more than five to ten days later), and we will get back to you by then.

Second, in the case of a promising candidate, after you've finished asking your questions, give the candidate an opportunity to ask you questions. But the key is, be brief. Save the details for the in-house interview. After the promising candidate has asked one or two questions, wrap up the call with the same closing script as above.

Now that you've completed the phone interviews and identified perhaps two or three solid candidates, it's time for an in-house interview. Here's what we'd like you to do during this interview.

First, ask each candidate to complete a short application that asks for a little more background information that's over and above what is listed on their résumé. For example, this would include such things as specific dates for previous employment, supervisor's name, educational history with degrees obtained, grade point average, and references. Also, have each sign a credit check authorization. This gives you the ability to check their background through one of the major credit bureaus but, there's no need to run the credit check now; you can save that for the person to whom you want to make an offer. See Figure 7.4 for an example.

Second, put candidates at ease early in the interview process. Give them an enthusiastic welcome and make small talk briefly about the weather or traffic or similar common topic. After that, get down to business. We like to begin the interview by telling candidates exactly what they can expect during the interview. For example:

John, here's what's going to happen over the next (you fill in the time period). I'll begin by asking you a series of questions and then I'll give you an opportunity to ask me some questions. At that point, I'll ask you to complete a short exercise on setting priorities, and I'll leave the room for a few minutes. But don't worry, there are no right or wrong answers to the exercise. When I come back, we'll discuss the exercise, and then I'll wrap things up by letting you know what the next step is.

FIGURE 7.4 *Authorization/Release Form for Background Checks*

I hereby authorize _____ to conduct a comprehensive review of my background causing a consumer report and/or an investigative consumer report to be generated for employment purposes. I understand that the scope of the consumer report/investigative consumer report may include, but is not limited to, the following areas:

> Verification of Social Security number; current and previous residences; employment history including all personnel files; education including transcripts; character references; credit history and reports; criminal history records from any criminal justice agency in any or all federal, state, county jurisdictions; birth records; motor vehicle records to include traffic citations and registration; and any other public records or to conduct interviews with third parties relative to my character or general reputation.

I further authorize any individual, company, firm, corporation, or public agency (including the Social Security Administration and law enforcement agencies) to divulge any and all information, verbal or written, pertaining to me to _____. I further authorize the complete release of any records or data pertaining to me that the individual, company, firm, corporation, or public agency may have, to include information or data received from other sources.

I hereby release _____, the Social Security Administration, and its agents, officials, representatives, or assigned agencies, including officers, employees, or related personnel both individually and collectively, from any and all liability for damages of whatever kind, which may, at any time, result to me, my heirs, family, or associates because of compliance with this authorization and request to release. You may contact me as indicated below.

Print Name: _____
First   Middle   Last   Maiden

Current Address: _____
Street   City   Zip / State

Social Security Number: _____

Date of Birth: _____

Home Telephone number: _____

Driver's License Number/State: _____

Signature: _____

Date: _____

Being interviewed can be very stressful and causes some people to behave much differently than they would in a normal, day-to-day working environment. You should strive to make candidates feel comfortable and welcome. By doing so, you'll get a truer picture of what each candidate is really like.

Third, don't tell candidates too much about the job before you ask your interview questions. All too often, unskilled interviewers begin by describing the available position. That's a mistake because it allows interviewees to structure their responses to fit the position. You want honest answers, not ones that are custom-tailored to what you want to hear.

Fourth, describe your mission, your vision, and your culture. As you're interviewing candidates, they're also interviewing you. You want to make sure that a candidate makes a good decision in wanting to come work with you. If you think a candidate is going to be the greatest employee in the world but doesn't think that positively about your firm, there's a mismatch. This mismatch can manifest itself in poor work results or quick turnover. One way to minimize this problem is to share your firm's mission, vision, and culture. Let the candidate know what it's like working at your company so he or she can make an informed decision about working with you should you decide to offer this person the position.

Fifth, be observant during the interview. You'd be surprised how many judgments you can make about a candidate if you consciously stay aware during the interview. Here are a few to consider:

- *Self-confidence.* As you ask candidates questions, do they respond with confidence or are they tentative?
- *Attitude.* You don't want employees with attitude problems. Much of our work involves interpersonal communication so an employee with a bad attitude is not going to cut it. During the interview, try to discern if the candidate is a happy person. Does the candidate seem to have a positive attitude? Do you feel like he or she would be fun to have around?

Most advisors have small offices so one bad apple in the group can make it bad for everyone.

- *Appearance and manners.* Do the candidates present themselves well? Were they dressed appropriately? We had one female candidate arrive in an outfit more appropriate for a Saturday night out on the town. Were they well groomed? Did they exhibit appropriate manners? One candidate came in for an interview and immediately grabbed a soft drink and a chocolate chip cookie. When the Peak staff member came out to greet her, she was still chewing and had to brush her hands together to get rid of the crumbs. It wasn't what we'd call a positive first impression.

- *Presence and poise.* Is this someone you would be proud to put in front of your clients? Does the candidate have the poise to deal with high net worth clients? If a candidate is nervous during the interview, don't expect that to change much once he or she is on the job and in front of big clients.

- *Handshake.* Did the candidates eagerly extend their hand and give you a firm handshake? If so, that's a positive sign of confidence. If their handshake was soft and tentative, look out.

- *Body language.* During the interview, watch what kind of signals candidates are sending? Are they sitting on the edge of their chair and leaning forward a little bit, which suggests they're really interested in what you are saying? Or are they slumped back in their chair? Are their shoulders hunched?

- *Relevant questions.* When they ask you a question, is it a reasonable, logical one based on the conversation you were just having with them or did it just come out of left field? Are they asking a question that you already answered earlier in the conversation? If they don't ask relevant questions or they ask questions about things you've already answered, it may suggest they're not paying attention.

- *Promptness.* Were they on time for the interview? Being late without a good reason is a big negative.
- *Initiative.* Look for any signals that would suggest a candidate is a self-starter. Your life will be much easier if your staff takes the initiative to get the job done instead of waiting for you to tell them what to do.
- *Responsibility.* Do they take responsibility for their actions? We're all going to make mistakes. We want staff members who are willing to take responsibility when they make a mistake and then take responsibility to fix it.

Sixth, ask each candidate to deliver a short presentation. No matter what position you're trying to fill, the candidate needs good communication skills. Sometimes we'll ask candidates to give an impromptu presentation on something they should have knowledge about. For example, if the candidate is presently in a sales position, we'll ask him or her to deliver a "sales pitch" for us. Other times we'll give candidates a topic two or three days in advance and ask them to put together a five-minute presentation. This will also tell you just how serious they are about working for you. If they decline to give the presentation, then you know they're either not very serious about your job or they lack the skills necessary to complete it.

Seventh, role-play with your candidates about a situation that is similar to the actual job they would perform. For example, let's say you're hiring a Director of First Impression. To test their skills in this area, you could create the following scenario:

You're the client and you've just walked in the door to the office. The advisor you're supposed to meet with won't be available for five more minutes. The candidate is the Director of First Impression and her job is to engage you in conversation for the next five minutes.

This simple role-playing could help you quickly determine the candidate's interpersonal skills, sincerity, and ability to think quickly.

If you're hiring an Associate Wealth Advisor, you might want to role-play a sales situation. For example, pick a sales situation that the candidate is knowledgeable about and then pretend you're a prospect. Ask the candidate to go through the process he or she would use to try and sell you on the product or service. As a variation, ask him or her to role-play this scenario not with you but with one of your staff members with whom the candidate hasn't yet met. This variation will help you determine the candidate's comfort level in talking to strangers.

Eighth, get a writing sample from the candidate. Sure, you have a résumé and a cover letter but how can you be confident the candidate wrote it? You certainly don't want grammatical errors or misspelled words on letters or e-mails that go to clients and prospects. To help us ensure our candidates have solid writing skills, we like to have each of our candidates give us a writing sample during the interview process. To do this, we typically ask the candidates to write down their answer to the following question: "What do you need to accomplish over the next ten years to consider yourself successful?" We then leave the room and give them about ten minutes to answer. Once they've completed it, we ask them to read it, and then we ask them some questions based on what they wrote.

Ninth, determine the candidates' client service aptitude. We've developed a short exercise (see Figure 7.5) with a series of customer service scenarios. Each scenario describes a typical situation that our office faces. We ask each candidate to prioritize the list. There's really no right or wrong answer. Our goal is to see how they decide what's most important and what's least important. After they've completed the exercise, we ask them to explain their reasoning. This exercise helps us identify how our candidates think and helps us discern their attitude toward client service.

FIGURE 7.5 *Client Service Aptitude Test*

Please prioritize the list below from 1 to 12 with 1 being the activity you would do first.

_____ Client calls with a change of address that will be in effect in five days.

_____ Client calls with a request for a payout from his account. The money is going to be used next month for a down payment on a car.

_____ Client calls to request that we send our current newsletter to an out-of-town son or daughter.

_____ Client calls the office to sell stock in her account. It's 2:30. and the market closes for the day at 3:00.

_____ Client calls and gives us a referral. This referral is the CEO of a Fortune 500 company. He is only going to be in Omaha for the day and would like to visit with us.

_____ Quarterly statements arrive and need to be put in client files.

_____ Client calls and requests some information to take to her accountant. Her meeting is in three business days.

_____ Client calls to make a beneficiary change in his account. The client is in the last stages of a terminal illness.

_____ Client wants to reschedule an appointment. The appointment is in two weeks and she wants to make it for three weeks out.

_____ We run out of client packets. New packets need to be assembled by Monday (today is Friday) to keep up with demand from prospects from the radio program.

_____ One of our biggest clients has stopped in the office unexpectedly with some questions about his account.

_____ A very important client has called you for information about his account and you have him on hold.

So now you've completed the first interview, and you've narrowed it down to one or two candidates. At this point, we'd encourage you to do a second interview, but this time make it a group interview. There are several benefits to this.

First, you can spend more time observing the candidate. As your colleagues ask questions, you can focus on the candidate, analyze his or her gestures, and ponder his or her responses.

Second, you can determine how the candidate handles pressure. A one-on-one interview is difficult, but being interviewed by a group turns up the pressure a few more notches. Does the candidate wilt or shine?

Third, you get a better sense of how the candidate interacts with a diverse group of people. Perhaps you and the candidate really clicked during your one-on-one interview, but how does the candidate react with the rest of your staff? The candidate needs to click with everybody or else he or she probably won't work out.

One of Steve's group interviews resulted in a homerun hire:

I interviewed a candidate who looked great on paper and performed well during the phone interview, so I brought him in for an interview. He was impressive in person but appeared to have a chip on his shoulder. Everything else looked good. He was articulate. He had great experience and the right temperament for the job. The only problem was, he just didn't seem like a very happy person. Not wanting to dismiss him at that point, I decided to bring him back for a group interview. There were four of us in the room interviewing him, and the result was very interesting. He came to the interview with a bright tie and a very positive attitude; he was extremely articulate and not flustered at all. He answered everybody's questions and made great eye contact. Afterward, I polled our interview group, and the conclusion was a resounding "Hire him." So I did, and he turned out to be a great hire who is still with the company today.

You might also consider taking candidates to lunch to see what social skills they have. If you do client events, you'll be around food, so it's good to know that your staff members can conduct themselves appropriately.

We've talked conceptually about the first and second interview; now it's time to get specific regarding the questions you should ask during these interviews.

As you well know from your experience meeting with prospective clients, asking the right questions can make all the difference in the world. It's no different when you're interviewing potential staff members.

Here are 11 questions you may want to ask:

1. *Question:* How would your childhood friends describe you?
   Comment: Although this may seem a strange question, it's really not. Because we're in a relationship business, this question tells you whether the candidate has been able to build long-term relationships. If the candidate still has childhood friends that he or she communicates with, that's a great sign.

2. *Question:* If I picked up the phone and called your last supervisor, what would he or she say about you?
   Comment: You usually get a pretty honest answer to this question because the candidate is thinking, "I better be honest here because the interviewer may give my last supervisor a call." How candidates answer this question also helps you determine not just candidates' perception of themselves but also a third-party's perception of the candidates.

3. *Question:* Describe a situation in which you set a goal and tell how you achieved it.
   Comment: If candidates don't have a good answer to this, it may suggest they're not a goal-setting type of person, and that could be a problem.

4. *Question:* What new skills have you learned in the past 12 months?
   Comment: We like to hire people who are learning new things and continuing to grow. If they can't tell us anything they've learned in the last 12 months, they may be more

interested in defending what they know instead of embracing what they don't know.

5. *Question*: Who are your heroes and why?

   Comment: You can learn a lot about a person by simply knowing who they look up to and why. It gives you more insight into what makes a person tick and what his or her values are.

6. *Question:* What have you been criticized for, and what did you do about it?

   Comment: Most interviewers typically ask candidates to discuss their strengths and weaknesses. Candidates are usually prepared for this question so they typically turn their weakness into a positive. But when you ask them a direct question, such as "What have you been criticized for?" it's really hard for them to weasel their way out of it. By following up with "What did you do about it?" you can determine if they took the criticism constructively and did something about it.

7. *Question:* Tell me about a work situation that bugged you.

   Comment: All of us have our idiosyncrasies, and this is the kind of question that's going to bring some of them out. Depending on the answer, it might bring out a potential problem of culture fit that needs to be explored further.

8. *Question:* What will you do in the future that you have not been willing to do in the past in order to be successful?

   Comment: It's a positive sign if candidates can readily identify something they're willing to do now in order to excel at your firm. A good answer might be: "I'm willing to work extra hours if necessary, whereas in the past my hours had to be fixed because of my kids' schedules.

9. *Question:* What is your most significant business accomplishment?

   Comment: After candidates tell you what the accomplishment is, ask them to describe all the details about the accomplishment. You should be keeping your eyes and ears open for several things here. First, they should be extremely positive and enthusiastic as they describe the accomplishment; after all, it's the one they're most proud of. And, second, you should determine if the skills required for that accomplishment are transferable to your position.

10. *Question:* Are you lucky?

   Comment: Our experience suggests people who say, "Yes, I'm a lucky person," are generally positive, grateful people. Those who say, "No, I'm unlucky," tend to be more negative. Let them take their bad luck to somebody else's company.

11. *Question:* Why should we choose you?

   Comment: This is a catchall question that gives candidates a real opportunity to sell themselves. And if they are not strong and positive when they respond to this question, that's a concern. We want someone who's a little bit aggressive, who's confident. You want to hear them say something like:

   > You should choose me because I have excellent skills, vast knowledge, and a great attitude. I work well with people, and I really like what I see in your company. I've spent a lot of time researching your organization and I've found nothing but positive things. I'm really excited about the people I've met here, and I think I could really make a significant contribution to your organization.

   That type of response is indicative of the attitude you want your new hires to have.

The following is a long list of interview questions. Go through the list, pick a few questions that resonate with you, and then add them to your interviewing process.

Possible Interview Questions

1. Tell me what you know about our organization.

2. Based on what you know about this position, what characteristics would you look for in the person filling this position?

3. What did a typical day look like in your previous position?

4. What achievements were you most proud of in your last position?

5. What activities did you enjoy the most in your last position?

6. Why are you looking for a new position?

7. What did you like/dislike about your last supervisor?

8. If I asked your last supervisor to describe your work habits, what would he or she say?

9. How do you like interacting with your supervisor? Describe the worst supervisor you ever worked for.

10. What's the nicest compliment you've ever received and why did you receive it?

11. In your last performance review, what area did your supervisor say you needed to improve?

12. What have you accomplished that is unusual?

13. What personal and professional achievements are you most proud of and why?

14. What are some of your goals away from the office?

15. What are your professional goals over the next five to ten years?

16. What new skills have you learned in the past 12 months? What would you like to learn in the next year?

17. Describe a significant change in your job responsibilities and the steps you took to manage the transition smoothly.

18. Tell me about a situation when you abruptly had to change what you were doing.

19. Tell me about a time when you worked on a project that did not turn out well. How did you handle that?

20. When you take on a new project, do you like to have lots of guidance and feedback up front, or do you prefer to try your own approach?

21. Describe a time when you felt it necessary to modify or change your actions in order to respond to the needs of another person.

22. What kinds of people do you not enjoy working with?

23. Tell me about a work situation that bugged you.

24. Describe a problem that you confronted without success. If you could go back in time, how would you handle it differently?

25. Give an example of the most significant problem you have faced and solved at work. Describe the process you used to find a solution.

26. Tell me about the most difficult coworker you ever worked with. What actions did you take that proved helpful? What did you realize made things worse? What would you do differently if you were faced with a similar situation in the future?

27. Describe the most creative, work-related project you have done.

28. Give me an example of a time when you had an unusual idea that worked well.

29. When was the last time you "broke" the rules, and what did you do?

30. What is the most interesting thing you have done in the past year?

31. What would you do if you were asked to take on an exciting new project that you really wanted to do but you already had more work than you could handle?

32. Based on your current level of knowledge about this position, describe your level of interest.

33. What are some of the strengths you utilize in your current work that can help you in this position?

34. Have you ever experienced a personal loss from doing what is right?

35. In what business situations do you feel honesty would be inappropriate?

36. Describe a situation when you were faced with making a decision that involved important conflicting needs between an individual and your employer and explain how you handled it.

37. Review your accomplishments for the past five years. What do you think are the main qualities, characteristics, and strengths that enabled you to do well?

38. What are the things you like to do the most in your spare time?

39. What qualities do people admire in you?

40. Describe a project or idea that initially met resistance but that you were able to "sell" to others and implement.

41. Tell me about a time when you disagreed with the others in a group about something important but were able to work with them to reach a consensus that you felt was a good one.

42. How have you handled a situation when you needed to "correct" your boss?

43. What question would you like me to ask you that I haven't already asked?

44. Why should we choose you?

During the interview, you should take a few notes. Immediately after the interview, evaluate your notes, write a summary, and then determine your next step. If you're not going to make an offer, then send the applicant a polite turndown letter. If you are ready to make an offer, then move to Step #5—make the offer.

Step #5. Make the Offer

The first thing we'd like you to do is pick up the phone, call the candidate, and let him or her know that you are planning on making an offer. Briefly state what the offer is and ask if he or she has any last-minute questions or comments. Reiterate how excited you are about the candidate possibly joining your firm. After you hang up, send the offer letter. You can send the offer via e-mail to get it there faster but also follow that up by sending it by regular mail.

The offer letter should clearly state the position, the benefits, the compensation, and the start date. Please see Figure 7.6 for an example.

Sometimes, the candidate will come back to you with a counteroffer. We had this happen to us twice in the past year. One time we raised our initial offer after hearing the candidate's logic, and it worked out great for us. The other time we declined to raise our offer and did not hire the candidate. This also worked out great for us because we found another candidate who fit even better. You're the only one who can judge whether you should raise your initial offer. Listen to the candidate's logic, carefully study how the candidate is conducting himself or herself in the process, and then make an informed decision.

After your candidate accepts the offer, make sure you get the workspace prepared ahead of time. The worst thing you can do is have a new employee start without a phone that's connected or a computer that works. Also make sure your new employee has a great workspace. You might think you're saving money by cramming people in like sardines, but what you save in rent, you'll more than lose in productivity.

We've developed the New Employee Checklist in Figure 7.7 that you may find helpful.

FIGURE 7.6 *Sample Offer Letter*

January 12, 2005

Jan Newhire
123 Abba Circle
Omaha, NE 68104

Dear Jan,

We are all very much impressed with your skills and experience and would like to offer you a position with Peak Productions as our Director of First Impression. This is a full-time position with traditional working hours. Your supervisor would be Melinda Greatemployee, who is our Team Leader.

Peak Productions offers health benefits through Great Healthcare Company. Peak Productions covers 100 percent of the premium for the employee, and any additional premium is paid by the employee. We also offer a 401(k) plan with up to a 6 percent company match. There is a one-year waiting period to become eligible. We also recognize seven paid holidays and offer a PTO program that starts with 9 PTO days in your first year and ramps up to 20 PTO days beginning in year six.

The compensation is as follows:

• Base salary of $24,000,
• An annual bonus of $7,000 (paid quarterly) based on meeting agreed-upon quarterly goals.

We would like you to start February 2, 2005.

Jan, I hope you'll accept our offer, and I know you'll enjoy working here. There are tremendous opportunities that await you. You can reach me at (xxx) xxx-xxxx, and I look forward to hearing from you soon.

Sincerely,

Great Advisor

Great Advisor, CFP®

FIGURE 7.7 *New Employee Checklist*

Employee name _____

- ☐ Assign security key . . . . [Name of Person Responsible]
- ☐ Add to e-mail list . . . . [Name of Person Responsible]
- ☐ Add network log on name . . . . [Name of Person Responsible]
- ☐ Add phone extension and group mailbox . . [Name of Person Responsible]
- ☐ Update Welcome Letter for client
     notebook. . . . . [Name of Person Responsible]
- ☐ Update phone directory list. . . . . [Name of Person Responsible]
- ☐ Add bio to Web page . . . . [Name of Person Responsible]
- ☐ Add information to newsletter . . . . [Name of Person Responsible]
- ☐ Add name to marquee in lobby . . . . [Name of Person Responsible]
- ☐ Add to payroll and set up insurance
     deductions. . . . . [Name of Person Responsible]
- ☐ Discuss 401(k) benefits. . . . . [Name of Person Responsible]
- ☐ Add to Broker Dealer software
     subscription (when necessary). . . . . [Name of Person Responsible]
- ☐ Order business cards . . . . [Name of Person Responsible]
- ☐ Provide with a new Assistant's
     Workbook. . . . . [Name of Person Responsible]
- ☐ Train on Goldmine® . . . . [Name of Person Responsible]
- ☐ Train on Broker Dealer software. . . . . [Name of Person Responsible]
- ☐ Complete insurance worksheet. . . . . [Name of Person Responsible]
- ☐ Train on phone system . . . . [Name of Person Responsible]
- ☐ Set up PC workstation and e-mail address . [Name of Person Responsible]
- ☐ Read office copy of "Raving Fans" . . . . [Name of Person Responsible]
- ☐ Order office supplies . . . . [Name of Person Responsible]

Once this checklist is completed, return it to the supervisor, who will save it in the new employee's file.

ADDITIONAL THOUGHTS ON THE HIRING PROCESS

- It's still an art form. You can go through all these steps and think you're doing everything right, but in the end there's still some art to it. What's your gut feeling about the candidate? We had a situation one time where we hired a salesperson despite the lukewarm endorsement from a couple of our staff members. These two staff members just had an indefinable feeling about the candidate that left them uneasy about making an offer. Sure enough, after six days on the job, the new employee gave a bizarre reason for saying he couldn't work at our firm and quit. So if you have any nagging thoughts about a candidate, pay attention to them. If you can't resolve the thoughts, then move on to the next candidate.

- Try before you buy. What happens if you have two or more candidates and you can't decide which to choose? Have them each spend a day in your office. One time, Ron had three candidates who were virtually deadlocked, so he brought them in at separate times to work for him for a day. One of the candidates really stood out. Ron hired her, and she spent ten years with him before retiring as one of his best employees ever.

- Hire for attitude and train for skill. It's much easier to train someone to do a particular job than it is to take someone who knows how to do that job but has the wrong attitude. So if you find a candidate who's got the right attitude, the desire, the motivation, and the communication skills you're looking for but is a little short on experience, give that candidate a strong look anyway. If you've got a good gut feeling about a person and all that's missing is some experience, it might be wise to hire the person and invest a little time and money in training.

- Experienced candidates are not always the best candidates. Logically, it makes sense that you should hire people who have the experience you are looking for, but that's not always a great idea. For example, at Peak Productions we're very focused on delivering an extraordinary level of client service. We could hire someone from another firm who is experienced in client service, but it's possible that person's definition of client service could be much different from ours. At this person's old firm, acceptable client service might have been two notches below our standard of service, and it could be very hard for this person to change. So in some situations, you're better off starting with someone a little green and training him or her to your standards.

- It's better to be short-staffed than to hurry through the hiring process. It's very tempting to hire the first decent candidate who comes along when you're short-staffed. Unfortunately, a short-term solution may result in a long-term problem. Remember, if you want to have A+ clients, you have to have A+ staff. Take the extra time you need during the hiring process because it will pay big dividends in the long run. You'll end up saving money because you'll have less employee turnover, you'll have more productive employees, and you'll spend less time and money in training. For example, at Peak Productions, we spent nine months looking for a salesperson. During that period, we missed out on some revenue because we were short-staffed. But we waited until we found the right candidate, and once we did, our sales took off again.

- Don't hesitate to fire poor performers. If it becomes clear to you early on that your new hire is not what you expected, don't let the situation fester. Talk to the employee, express your concerns, describe what the person can do to improve, and if the situation does not get better, let the person go. All employees should be hired with the understanding that they're on a 90-day "probationary" period. You should know very clearly within 90 days if an employee is going to work out or not. Keeping an employee on staff who isn't working out not only hurts you but also hurts the employee, because it just delays his or her getting on with life.

If you follow this process, you'll end up with an A+ staff and be well positioned to grow your business substantially while at the same time maintaining a great quality of life.

SUMMARY

- If you want to attract and retain A+ and A clients and have a great quality of life, you have to have an A+ and A staff.
- Our philosophy is to hire staff people to do all the work that can be done for less than the average hourly wage.
- Think of your staff not as an expense but as an investment. Done well, your staff will be one of the best investments you ever make.
- When hiring new staff, follow this five-step process
    1. Evaluate your current staffing situation.
    2. Develop job descriptions.
    3. Search for candidates.
    4. Screen and interview candidates.
    5. Make the offer.

TNT #2 ACTION STEPS

- Create two organization charts. The first chart reflects your current staff, and the second chart reflects what you'd like your business to look like in the future when it's at your ideal level. Use this second chart as a guide to add additional staff.

- Review your existing staff and rate them as either A+, A, B, C, or D employees.

- If you have any C or D employees, let them go right away.

- If you have a B employee, develop a 90-day plan to either move him or her up to an A or A+ by restructuring the job and offering additional training or let the employee go.

- Implement a results-based pay compensation system.

- Follow the five steps to hiring an A+ staff if you need to hire new staff members.

SYSTEMATIZE EVERYTHING

8

ELEVATE YOUR SERVICE BY FOLLOWING THE SYSTEM

"Don't agonize. Organize."

—FLORENCE KENNEDY

It's no secret that poor service abounds in our society, and much of it stems from a lack of systemization. Witness what happened to Steve recently.

I was standing in line at the checkout counter of a health food store when two little kids came running around the corner. The checkout person was not amused and curtly said, "Kids, no running; I don't want you to get hurt." About ten seconds later, the kids' mom appeared just in time to hear the kids let out a little scream and to hear the checkout person scold them with this little gem, "Hey, this is a business; you can't do that in here." None too pleased, the mother grabbed her kids and stormed out the door saying, "I'll do my shopping on the Internet from now on."

About a minute later, another store employee came out from the back room and asked the checkout person where the lady (the mom) that he was helping went. The checkout person said she left. Unable to resist, I commented, "She said she'll do her shopping on the Internet going forward." And with one last jab, the checkout person said, "That's good; she needs to do a better job controlling her kids." This was all within earshot of two other customers.

The checkout person still didn't get it. She thought the mom would go to her store's Web site to buy her products, but instead, the checkout person just lost for the store a customer for life because of her poor response to the situation.

Clearly, this store didn't have a good customer service training system in place. Imagine how differently the situation could have turned out had the checkout person handled the situation with more diplomacy. Instead of losing a customer for life, the checkout person could have created a frenzied fan who told all her friends about the great health food store with the friendly staff that gracefully handled a couple of rambunctious kids.

All it would have taken to win a customer for life was a simple system for dealing with loud, energetic kids. Because no system was in place, the store clerk resorted to her own poor instincts and made the situation worse.

THE BENEFITS OF SYSTEMS

There are four major benefits to systematizing your office:

1. *You can offer the best service and be the lowest cost provider.* The airline industry is a good example. There's a wide disparity in the level of service and profitability of the nation's major airlines. Especially since 9/11, most fliers dread the thought of having to get on a plane for fear of rude flight attendants, lost luggage, delayed or cancelled flights, and long lines. But there are a few airlines that seem to have found the right formula.

According to the Airline Quality Rating 2004 Report, three of the top four airlines are low-cost carriers. Why? According to the study's authors, the low-cost airlines are on time more often, they bump fewer passengers, they mishandle less baggage, and they generate fewer complaints. So how do Jet Blue, Southwest, and America West keep costs low yet still provide great service in an industry notorious for poor performance? In a word—systems.

Here are some examples of how Southwest Airlines keeps costs low but service high.

- Southwest flies only one type of plane, a Boeing 737. That's extremely efficient because its mechanics have to be trained only on repairing one type of plane, its pilots have to be trained only on how to fly one type of plane, and all planes are interchangeable on every route.

- The airline doesn't have assigned seats. The infamous Southwest "cattle call" ain't pretty, but it's efficient. By eliminating assigned seats, Southwest saves ten minutes on the ground, which allows it to turn its planes around faster and add millions of dollars to the bottom line each year.

- Southwest doesn't participate in the major online reservation systems but Southwest uses its own simplified online reservation system that saves it millions of dollars a year in transaction fees.

The three operating strategies outlined above don't fit into a Systems Manual. However, they fit into a systems philosophy of keeping costs low and service high. A good question to ask yourself and your team on a periodic basis is, "How can we do things better, faster, simpler, and more profitably?" Southwest and the other top-performing, low-cost airlines have asked that question repeatedly and answered it emphatically.

2. *You can be more efficient, which will lead to higher profits and an improved quality of life.* This efficiency increase allows you to get more done in less time and with greater accuracy. The days of spending long hours at the office scratching your head thinking about how to do something or redoing things that weren't done right in the first place will be long gone.

3. *Your office will commit fewer errors.* By having a written system, your staff will have a guide to follow that clearly explains how to do each task in your office. There should be no more excuses for errors.

4. *You can get new staff trained faster and up and running more quickly.* Training staff is usually not high on an advisor's priority list. However, it's extremely important that your office is full of highly qualified A+ or A staff members. Use your Systems Manual as a training manual for new staff members. Require them to keep the manual on their desk and refer to it as they go about learning their daily activities. With the manual as a guide, there should be fewer errors, and the new staff member will have a more positive learning experience.

Small Improvements Can Make a Big Difference

In the financial advisory business, it's a winner-take-all scenario. Either you get the account or you don't. But just imagine if you could make some small improvements in your practice that would lead to big profits in your business. Would you work on those small improvements? Of course you would. Pro golfers are a great example of this phenomenon of small improvements leading to big profits.

In 2003, pro golfer Davis Love III won $6,081,896 in prize money on the PGA Tour and had a per round stroke average of

69.41. Far down the leader board was Mike Sposa, an unknown, unheralded pro who won $276,447 and had a per round stroke average of 71.35.

Notice that Love shot only two strokes per round better than Sposa yet he won 22 times more money. Love's two-stroke margin translates into just a 3 percent advantage, but in the money column, it translates into a 2,100 percent advantage—and that doesn't even include endorsement money.

Just think, one missed putt or one wayward tee shot every nine holes made the difference between multi-million-dollar riches and marginal obscurity. It's the same in our business. One poor first impression, one ill-timed comment, or one neglected proactive phone call each week could be the difference between the President's Club and the Pauper's Club.

Take a moment and look around your business. Can you find ways to make a 3 percent improvement? How difficult would it be to:

- Increase your referrals by 3 percent?
- Add 3 percent more clients?
- Get 3 percent more of your current clients' total assets?
- Reduce your expenses by 3 percent?
- Reduce your client turnover by 3 percent?
- Get your staff to give 3 percent more effort?
- Improve your communication skills by 3 percent?
- Perform 3 percent more random acts of kindness for your clients?

It's not as difficult to do these things as you might think. It boils down to finding something that works and then systematizing it so you can repeat it on a consistent basis. For example, let's say you're meeting with a prospect, and in the course of the conversation you say something brilliant that really lights up the prospect. That's an insight that you need to be aware of and make part of your repertoire; and yes, it should be written down in the prospects section of your Systems Manual so you repeat it each time when appropriate.

It's the same for your staff. Remind them that they should be on the lookout for new and improved ways of completing tasks, communicating with clients and prospects, and elevating the level of service they provide. And when they find a new and improved way of doing something, make sure they document it in the Systems Manual.

When you have a systems mentality, you should be constantly tweaking every aspect of your business. Focus on making continuous improvements that will allow your business to stay ahead of the competition.

So how do you turn a new or better way of doing something into results? It's quite simple. Write up the idea into a system, put it in your Systems Manual, and follow it religiously.

The Japanese have a word called *Kaizen,* which means gradual, orderly, and continuous improvement. It applies not just to business but to life as well. If you adopt the philosophy of *Kaizen* and focus on making small but steady 3 percent gains, your incremental improvements will turn into quantum results. Before you know it, you'll have a Four Seasons practice with Southwest efficiency.

THE SYSTEM IS THE SOLUTION

Having a system allows you to deliver a high level of service on a consistent basis. How often has something come up in your practice when one of your staff members asked you, "How should we handle this?" With a system in place, your staff member would simply refer to the manual and see exactly how to handle it. In this environment, everybody wins. The client gets taken care of in a timely and consistent manner. The staff member feels confident because he or she has a readily available source to refer to when questions arise. And the advisor is more productive because he or she has fewer interruptions and fewer questions to answer. See Figure 8.1 for a list of the nine areas to be systematized.

So what exactly do we mean by a "system"? A system is a formalized mechanism that helps ensure you perform an activity according to a certain standard. For example, it could be a ritual

FIGURE 8.1 *The Nine Areas to Be Systematized*

The Nine Areas to Be Systematized

1. Prospects & Referrals—systems for information packets, entering data into your contact management system, follow-up procedures, turndown letters, thank-you letters, appointment confirmation letters, developing proposals, prospect meeting agenda and questions to ask, summarizing meetings
2. New Clients—systems for welcome packets, client profile sheets, listing of services provided, processing business, welcome aboard card, thank-you letter, setting up new client file, entering into contact management system, allocating assets, putting together client notebook, disclosure statements, overview of new and existing client meetings
3. Transfers—systems for ACAT overview, non-ACAT overview, copying business, overnight business, proprietary assets liquidation letter, annuity transfers, journaling between accounts, outgoing accounts exit letter, outgoing accounts survey
4. Trading—systems for equity, mutual fund, fixed income, and option trades, exchanges, trading errors, margin accounts, block trading, prospectus receipts, switch letters
5. Client Service—systems for appointments, sending reminders, greeting clients, phone scripts, referral request letters, check processing, address changes, annual surveys, death claims, closing or changing accounts, surrenders and redemptions, saving business records, client complaints, client follow-up, firing a client, market fluctuation letter, saving business records, things you need to understand about your portfolio letter, urgent business envelopes
6. Updates—systems for portfolio updates, online account access, update letters, update books
7. Client Appreciation—systems for client events (budgets, checklists, supplies, agendas, food and drink, ideas, name tags, sign-in, and evaluation), birthday and gift vendors, Love Affair Marketing, newsletter publication timeline, prospects attending workshops, compliance issues, RSVPs, special mailings
8. Office Procedures—systems for meeting agendas, checking files in or out, correspondence files, group e-mails, front desk a.m. and p.m. procedures, literature room, money line reports, six most important, team meetings, wall calendar, workout schedule
9. Human Resources—procedures for authorizing a background check, confidentiality agreements, employee handbook, employee exit checklist, new advisor checklist, new employee checklist, out-of-office e-mail procedures, part-time and temporary help, sample interview questions and test, staff member leaving work early, staff member not coming in, vacation days

that you perform on a regular basis such as reading your mission and vision each morning. It could be a written procedure that details exactly how to open a new brokerage account. Or it could be a checklist that outlines the specific steps necessary to accomplish a particular task.

Ultimately, each staff member should have his or her own copy of the office Systems Manual. This manual could be a three-ring binder with nine tabs (see Figure 8.1). Each tab would contain the appropriate procedures, checklists, and forms for that specific area. Keeping the manual handy and up-to-date makes it easy for your staff to follow procedures and deliver a high level of service on a consistent basis.

Creating your own Systems Manual is critical to building a world-class financial services business. Without one, you'll be winging it and forever stuck in low gear. Unfortunately, creating a Systems Manual is a time-consuming, labor-intensive activity. To aid you, Peak Productions has created a sample Systems Manual that you can purchase from us and then customize for your office. It comes complete with the nine tabs mentioned in Figure 8.1 along with a CD that contains electronic versions of the systems.

If you want to create your manual from scratch, here are the five steps you should follow:

1. Complete your mission and vision. If you're not systematized, it's not because you're too lazy or too distracted; it's because you haven't given yourself a compelling enough reason to get systematized. You haven't connected the benefit of systemization with your ultimate compelling reason, which is your mission and vision. If you have a mission and a vision that you fully connect with and that give you energy and motivate you to take action, then you'll find the time to get your office systematized, because doing so is a crucial move that allows you to have the quality of life you're looking for. That's one more great reason to have a

mission and vision; they motivate you to do the things you know you have to do to get closer to your mission and vision. And that's true for systemization or any other activity that you're procrastinating about. If you don't have a compelling enough reason to do it, it won't get done. So always ask yourself, how does completing this activity get me closer to my mission and vision? If the answer is, it doesn't, then you shouldn't do it. If it does get you closer to your mission and vision yet you still don't want to do it, then either you truly are lazy or, more likely, you need to rework your mission and vision because they're not compelling enough to persuade you to take action. We can't stress to you enough how important it is for you to develop your own personalized mission and vision that you fully connect with and that become a motivating document for you.

2. Commit to systematizing your office by making it a goal. We talked about goal-setting earlier and how important it is to set goals that are specific, measurable, achievable, and compatible. Systematizing your office fits that classic definition. By making that a goal, you'll dramatically increase the odds of its actually happening.

3. Thoroughly discuss the systemization process with your key staff person(s). To jump-start the process, you need to designate a key person in your office to spearhead the effort. Here's what you should discuss with this person.

   First, explain your goal. Let the person know that your goal is to have a system for every activity and a complete, customized, written Systems Manual. The manual is the tangible end product that you're striving for.

   Second, explain the process that you'd like the associate to follow to get the systems written and implemented. The key here is to not get overwhelmed. Going from little or no systems today to a fully systematized office can be a daunting task, but like all big projects, you need to start one step at a time. Our Systems Manual is set up in nine categories or tabs as follows:

1. Prospects and Referrals
2. New Clients
3. Transfers
4. Trading
5. Client Service
6. Updates
7. Client Appreciation
8. Office Procedures
9. Human Resources

We recommend that you start systematizing one tab at a time. Start with #1 above and work your way through #9. See Figure 8.2 for examples of the activities within each tab for which you should have a system.

Third, review a few sample systems to make sure your key staff person is clear on what your expectations are. See the Sample Systems section later in this chapter for an example of one system from each of the nine sections.

Fourth, set weekly meetings with your key staff person and set deadlines to complete each tab. Monitoring the progress of getting the systems written is important. This allows you to review each system as it's written to make sure it's what you are expecting.

4. Make systemization part of your bonus plan. Earlier we talked about Ron's results-based pay and the bonus compensation plan. Systemization fits into that program very well. For example, you can tie systematizing the nine tabs into the bonus program. You may set a goal of completing three tabs per quarter so that in nine months you'll have your entire office systematized. Also, the bonus can cut two ways. If you have a system breakdown because a written system wasn't followed, you can reduce the quarterly bonus by 5 percent. And to prevent your staff from becoming

FIGURE 8.2 *Examples of Activities for Which You Should Have a System*

Prospects and Referrals Tab
Prospect and Referral Packets
Prospect and Referral Follow-up Procedure
Prospect and Referral Follow-up Letter
Prospect Packet Letter
Referral Prospect Packet Letter
Referral Request Letter #1
Referral Request Letter #2
Referral Request Letter #3
Referral Thank-You #1
Referral Thank-You #2
Referral Thank-You #3
Prospect Turndown Letters
Prospect and Referral Appointment Confirmation
Prospect Appointment Sheet
Fifteen Questions for Potential Client
Reminder Form—Prospects
Reminder Form
Prospect Meeting Thank-You #1
Prospect Meeting Thank-You #2
Proposals for Prospects
Prospect Meeting Evaluation

New Clients
New Client Packet Checklist
Welcome Packet
New Client Packet General Information
Client Profile Sheet
Reminder Form—New Client
Overview of New and Existing Client Meeting
    Procedures
New Client Initial Processing
New Business Coordinator Checklist
Adding New Clients to Contact Management System
Welcome-Aboard Card
Thank-You Letter—New Client
Setting Up New Client Files
New Client Update
Notebook Checklist and Procedures
Notebook Welcome Letter

Transfers
ACAT Transfer Overview
Overnight Business

Proprietary Liquidation Letter
Transfer Process—Annuities
Updating Pending Report
Variable Annuity Policy Mailed to Client—Letter
Variable Annuity Policy Receipt
Journal Letter
Pending File Procedures
Pending Report Sample
Outgoing Accounts
Outgoing Accounts Exit Letter
Outgoing Accounts Survey

Trading
Trading Error System
Block Trading and Margin Accounts
Prospectus Receipts for Mutual Fund Purchases
Prospectus Letter #1
Prospectus Letter #2
Prospectus and Switch Letter #1
Prospectus and Switch Letter #2

Client Service
Customer Service Overview
Scheduling Overview
Appointment Scheduling Script
Reminder Form
Things You Need to Understand about Your
    Portfolio
Appointment Overview
    Appointment Sheet
    Referrals
    Market Fluctuation Acknowledgment
    Appointment Follow-up Letter—Market
        Volatility—Changes
    Appointment Follow-up Letter—Market
        Volatility—No Changes
Greeting Clients
Rep to Associate Client Move
Internal Broker Change Letter
Check Processing
Address Change
Address Change Request Form
Address Change—Letter to Companies

(continued)

FIGURE 8.2 *Examples of Activities for Which You Should Have a System, continued*

Client Service, continued
Annual Survey Overview
Annual Survey—2004
Annual Survey—Format Sample from Previous Years
Love Affair Marketing Survey
Death Claims
Closing or Changing Investment Contracts/ Accounts
Partial Surrenders or Redemptions
Urgent Business Labels
Business Records Envelope
Saving Business Records
Congratulations Certificate
Congratulations Certificate Form
Client Complaints—Written or Verbal
Transaction to Fee Structure Letter
Firing a Client—#1
Firing a Client—#2

Updates
Update System—New Client
Update—Existing Client
Portfolio Update Checklist (Training Version)
Portfolio Update Checklist (Condensed)
Sample Update
Sample Update Summary Calculations
Update Codes
Phone List for Fund Companies
Update Letters—Mailed Update
Update Letters—Need Appointment
Update Notebooks

Client Appreciation
Client Gifts Breakdown
Love Affair Marketing
Client Event Checklist
    Reservation Line for Client Events
Client Event Budget
Food/Drink Suggestions for Workshops
Client Events—Supplies
Client Event Name Tags
Client Event Agenda

Prospects Attending Workshop
Client Events Ideas
Required Material in File for Client Events
Newsletters
Newsletter Timeline
Special Mailings
Client Event Evaluation and Sign-in Overview
Introduction of Market Commentary

Office Procedures
Correspondence Files
Copytalk Letters and Checklist
Front Desk A.M. Checklist
Front Desk P.M. Checklist
The Literature Room
Literature Room Reorder Form
The Six Most Important Things to Do Tomorrow
Six Most Important Form
Team Meetings
Wall Calendar
Monthly Calendar
Checking Out/In a File
Agenda Procedures
Workout Schedule
Monthly Money Line Report
Individual Fund Company Deposits

Human Resources
New Employee Checklist
New Advisor Checklist
Employee Exit Checklist
Part-time Help
Quiz for Applicants
Sample Questions to Ask during an Interview
Team Member Leaving Early Checklist
Team Member Not Coming into Work
Vacation Days/Sick Days/Personal Days
Confidentiality Agreement
Authorization Form for Consumer Reports
    (background check)
Noncompete Agreement with Associate Advisors
Out-of-Office E-mail System

demoralized, you could also offer an opportunity to recoup that 5 percent by completing a special project or going above and beyond the call of duty in some other activity.

5. Add or revise your systems as needed. Systematizing your office is not a static process. You don't want to do it once and then forget about it. As time goes on, you may discover better or more efficient ways to do something, so your systems should be updated accordingly. And as you add new services or activities in your office, new systems should be written to cover them. By keeping your Systems Manual a living, breathing document, you'll get more benefit from it.

We fully realize that creating systems and monitoring their use is anathema to most advisors. It's no fun, it's hard work, and there's no immediate financial gratification. It's kind of like oatmeal. You may not like the taste of it, but it's sure good for you in the long run.

COMPREHENSIVE EXAMPLE OF A SYSTEM

You know you're in trouble when you have an annual review with a client, and you are just as surprised at the performance of the client's portfolio as the client is. Unfortunately, that happens too frequently. The problem occurs when you have no system for selecting and monitoring investments and reporting on their performance. Here's a detailed example of how you can fix that.

The first step is to refine your investment philosophy. What exactly do you believe in? Try to boil this down to one sentence. For example, your philosophy may be "The key to long-term investment success with acceptable risk is to develop a low-expense, globally diversified portfolio of equities, bonds, real estate, natural resources, and cash; and adjust it on a periodic basis to reflect current and expected economic conditions."

That's a pretty broad philosophy that leaves you room to maneuver as needed, but at least you now have a working thesis on which to build your portfolios.

Step two is to create several broadly diversified model portfolios. You may want to start with three portfolios—growth, growth and income, and income. Each of these three model portfolios should contain a mix of asset classes and should be weighted based on the objective of the model. For example, the growth model may contain 60 percent equities, 15 percent bonds, 10 percent real estate, 10 percent natural resources, and 5 percent cash. On the other hand, the income model might contain 10 percent equities, 70 percent bonds, 10 percent real estate, and 10 percent cash. To aid you in determining the appropriate allocation, consider purchasing an asset allocation software package. This will help eliminate some of the guesswork and move you closer to the most efficient portfolio for the level of risk you are targeting.

These models can be further divided into more specific asset classes. For example, the equity component can be segmented into large-cap growth, large-cap value, mid-cap growth, mid-cap value, small-cap growth, small-cap value, and emerging markets just to name a few. Your models should specify what allocation percentage you want for each of these asset classes.

So now you have three models with very specific asset allocations in each. Step three is to develop a system for selecting the investments you will use within each asset class. Here's where technology and software can help. A wide variety of investment selection software systems are on the market; which one you choose depends on your specific preferences. Regardless of which software system you choose, make sure it provides the ability to screen the database.

For example, let's say you are looking for a large-cap value mutual fund. To screen for such a fund, you need to determine which parameters are important to you. This could include screening for funds that have on average: a PE ratio less than 15, a price-to-book ratio less than 2, a dividend yield greater than 3, and so on. Once you home in on some promising candidates, you can use the Internet to do further research on these fund companies and even call the wholesalers to get additional information.

For each asset class in which you invest, you should have at least two mutual funds or exchange-traded funds on your buy list. If you focus on individual stocks, you should have at least five stocks on your buy list for each asset class.

Step four is to create a system for monitoring your asset allocation and your approved securities list. This can be done by inputting your approved securities in a Web-based portfolio tracker or by utilizing your broker-dealer's technology. The output you're looking for is a sheet that lists your approved securities by asset class along with their performance for the following periods: week, month, three months, year-to-date, one year, three years, five years, and ten years. Now you just have to review this list on a weekly basis, and you can easily track the performance of all your recommended securities. When one of your securities is performing out of line, you can quickly see that by comparing its performance to its asset class benchmark. Then you can readily decide if a change is needed.

Step five is creating a proposal system for communicating your process to prospects. You can save a tremendous amount of time by developing a standardized proposal that allows individual customization instead of creating a customized proposal for every prospect. Your proposal template should be a mix of standard language from a word-processing document, graphs inserted from your asset allocation software program, and customized data that are unique to that prospect. If you don't want to create your own proposal template, you can use an off-the-shelf financial planning or asset allocation software program.

There are two other things we'd like you to keep in mind. First, most of Ron's assets are managed on a discretionary basis, and that's very important because it increases office efficiency. When you have discretion, you don't have to contact every client each time you make a trade. That's a big time-saver when you are making an allocation shift or are swapping one security for another.

Having discretionary authority also helps in the sales process. When Ron delivers a proposal to a prospect, he shows the prospect the proposed asset allocation—not the specific investments he's recommending (unless, of course, it's a product that he does not have discretion over). By persuading the client to agree to the allocation, Ron avoids (in most cases) a discussion about "why you are picking this fund instead of that fund." Once a prospect agrees to the allocation and becomes a client, Ron invests his or her assets according to the model.

Second, if your clients' portfolios are presently scattered among a wide variety of investments, bite the bullet now and move as many of them as you can to one of the models you create. The sooner you can move your existing clients to your new model, the better off you and your clients will be.

By following these five steps, you can take the pain out of the asset management process and deliver a consistently positive experience to your clients.

OTHER SAMPLE SYSTEMS

Because systemization is such a critical component of successful financial advising, in Figure 8.3 we've listed an example of one system from each of the nine areas you should systematize. Remember, these systems should be aggregated in a Systems Manual and used on a daily basis by your staff.

FIGURE 8.3 *Prospect and Referrals (Used when a prospect asks for information about our firm)*

Prospect and Referral Follow-up System

1. Prospect packet is sent within 48 hours of receiving the request for information.
2. Scheduling manager enters prospect/referral data into the Contact Management System.
3. If the prospect was referred to us, send a thank-you note to the referrer. Enter and code the referral information into the Contact Management System.
4. Scheduling manager sets an appointment on the appropriate advisor's calendar to contact the prospect/referral ten days later to verify if the packet has been received and to see if the individual plans on returning it. Scheduling manager sets a "to do" on his or her calendar to follow up with the advisor 12 days later and ask the advisor about the progress of the prospect.
5. If the prospect/referral does not plan to return the packet:
   - The advisor thanks the prospect/referral for his or her time.
   - The advisor decides if the prospect should be added to the drip marketing list and, if so, notifies the Love Affair Marketing staff member.
   - If the prospect was a referral, the advisor contacts the referrer to let the referrer know there is no interest at this time.
   - No further contact will be made from our office.
6. If the prospect packet is returned to the scheduling manager:
   - The scheduling manager enters all information into the Contact Management System and then forwards the Confidential Personal and Financial Profile to the advisor.
   - The advisor reviews the information and lets the team know who returned a packet. This gives everyone a chance to see if they know any information about the prospect/referral that would be helpful in evaluating the packet.
   - If the prospect is accepted as a client, the scheduling manager schedules the appointment and codes it as an *initial appointment.*
   - If the prospect/referral is rejected as a potential client and the prospect is a referral, discuss with the advisor how to handle this delicate situation and make a determination. If the prospect is not a referral, send a turndown letter and return all the materials to the prospect; record the turndown in the Contact Management System, and change the Advisor field to "None."
   - Record the turndown in the Contact Management System and code as "Old" in the Advisor field, send a turndown letter, and return any materials to the referral. If this is the first referral received from a particular client, the advisor should probably work with the referral regardless of portfolio size. However, if the advisor has established minimums, it is important to call the client who made the referral and let that person know that the advisor made an exception in deciding to work with the referral. This is an excellent opportunity to train clients regarding the kind of referrals the advisor wants to receive. Let the client know that the advisor accepts a limited number of new clients each year to ensure that we can provide top service to existing clients. If the client continues to provide referrals that do not meet the minimum criteria, send a turndown letter and return all materials to the referral. Let the client know that we turned down his referral.

(continued)

FIGURE 8.3 *Prospect and Referrals (Used when a prospect asks for information about our firm), continued*

7. During the initial appointment, the Confidential Personal and Financial Profile is reviewed. Concerns are identified and an action plan is agreed upon. Any additional information and documents are discussed.

8. Following the initial meeting, the following letter is sent by the advisor thanking the prospect/referral for the appointment. This letter is used to recap the meeting and resembles the following.

Prospect and Referral Follow-up Letter

[Insert Date]

[Insert Prospect Name]
[Insert Prospect Address]

Dear [Insert Prospect Name],

I enjoyed meeting with you on [Insert Date] and would like to review the topics we discussed.

Points of Discussion:

- [Insert Points of Discussion]
- [Insert Points of Discussion]
- [Insert Points of Discussion]

Please let me know if any of the above items are incorrect.

Action Plan:

- [Insert Points for Action Plan]
- [Insert Points for Action Plan]
- [Insert Points for Action Plan]

If you have any other questions, please feel free to contact me by e-mail at [Insert E-mail Address] or call me at [Insert Phone Number].

Sincerely,

[Wealth Advisor Name]
Wealth Advisor

FIGURE 8.3 *Prospect and Referrals (Used when a prospect asks for information about our firm), continued*

9. A second meeting is scheduled to review the proposal and answer any remaining questions. A second follow-up letter is sent recapping this meeting as well. If the prospect agrees to become a client, a third meeting is scheduled for the client to come back and complete the account paperwork.

10. The advisor reviews the prospect/referral list every two months to determine who should be added to the "Drip" list. If no interest, code as "Old" in the Advisor field of the Contact Management System.

New Clients

Welcome-Aboard Card

The New Business Coordinator hand-writes the following message on specially designed note cards. The card is passed around the office for all team members to sign. The New Business Coordinator mails the card. Following is the content of the note:

Dear **[Insert New Client Name]**,

Thank you for choosing **[Insert Company Name]** for your investment needs. We know you will be pleased with our services. Your team is ready to assist you.

Sincerely,

All team members (including the advisor) sign the note that will be mailed within three days of the person's or couple's becoming clients.

Transfers

Non-ACAT Transfers

Non-ACAT transfers include transfers directly from mutual fund companies and certificates of deposit held at banks.

The advisor provides instructions on how to transfer the securities:

1. Transfer in-kind (the actual mutual funds, CDs, etc. will be transferred to the respective broker-dealer account). – OR –
2. Liquidate all assets and transfer as cash.

For non-ACAT transfers, signature-guarantee the transfer forms before sending them to your broker-dealer.

(continued)

FIGURE 8.3 *Prospect and Referrals (Used when a prospect asks for information about our firm), continued*

STEPS:

1. Forms Needed: Your Broker-Dealer New Account Application, your Broker-Dealer Customer Account Transfer Form, copy of current client statement. Complete all paperwork, including client and advisor's signatures and signature guarantee. Make a copy for the pending file with the date sent to your broker-dealer written on top. Record as pending in the Contact Manager System.

2. Overnight original materials to your broker-dealer. Transfers can take three to six weeks. Your broker-dealer can track this process.

3. Follow-up:

   a. Seven business days: Call your broker-dealer to verify receipt of paperwork and that the transfer is in the system.

   b. Twelve business days: Call your broker-dealer for a status report.

   c. Once you have a verification date of when the transfer will be completed, reference your online broker-dealer system to verify transfer was indeed completed.

   d. Throughout process: On a weekly basis, contact the client to apprise him or her of the status of the transfer until it's completed.

4. For the New Business Coordinator's own convenience: Check the client's account daily and print a snapshot of the account on the day the assets were received. This way you will already have the prices at which the shares transferred. These values will be used to prepare the initial update. And if this is a new client, these values establish the client account value at the time your company started advising the client.

5. Mark the transfer date and dollar amount of transfer on the front of the transfer form. Update the Contact Management System's pending to reflect a completed transfer.

6. Print a snapshot of the client account showing the transferred asset(s). Give the printout to the advisor. Call or e-mail the client to let him or her know the transfer is complete.

Trading

Trading Error System

When a trading error is discovered, act immediately to correct the mistake. Use the table below to keep a record of what happened.

FIGURE 8.3 *Prospect and Referrals (Used when a prospect asks for information about our firm), continued*

1. Contact the trade desk (equity or mutual fund).
2. Have a trader break all or a decided portion of trade.
3. If it was a mutual fund trade, contact the mutual fund company to find out what can be done on its end to help with the error (i.e., the cost).
4. Keep track of gain or loss—use any gain as leverage to break future trades not in our favor for no charge.
5. Keep track of contact people and conversations.
6. Once the gain or loss has been established, post it on the table and keep it in the error file.
7. Contact the client if confirmations will be sent. Explain that we caught the error quickly because we have a system for double-checking all trades.
8. Identify why the error occurred. Review the trading systems and make modifications if necessary.

Date	Contact Person	Original Trade Price	Busted Price	Gain or Loss	Total Gain or Loss

NOTES:

Client Service

Annual Survey Overview and CSI Index

Each year, at our year-end retreat, we decide what changes are necessary to the previous Annual Survey. Once decided, the new form is created and sent to Compliance for approval. Once it has been Compliance approved, the forms are printed internally.

Print the list of all A+ and A clients and mail a few surveys each week. To determine the number of surveys to send out weekly, divide the total number of A+ and A clients by the number of weeks in a year. They are mailed in alphabetical order.

Once a survey is returned, enter the rating as well as any additional information provided (e.g., e-mail address, referral, etc.) into the Contact Management System.

On a monthly basis, average the results and post the score in your office.

Sample Annual Survey

At [Insert Company Name], our goal is to continually improve our relationship with our clients. To reach this goal, we need your opinions and ideas. **Please complete this survey, refold it, and return it to us.**

(continued)

FIGURE 8.3 *Prospect and Referrals (Used when a prospect asks for information about our firm), continued*

On a scale of 1 to 10 (1 being low and 10 being high) please rate the following:

1. Are your phone calls to our office answered promptly and courteously by our receptionist?
   RATING: _____
   How important is this to you?
   RATING: _____

2. Are your phone calls promptly returned from our team?
   RATING: _____
   How important is this to you?
   RATING: _____

3. Are your questions answered to your satisfaction the first time?
   RATING: _____
   How important is this to you?
   RATING: _____

4. How would you rate the overall level of **SERVICE** received from your [Insert Co. Name] team?
   RATING: _____
   How important is this to you?
   RATING: _____

5. Our goal is to provide you with the **best customer service** experience you have ever had. Are we currently providing that? YES _____ NO _____

   If you answered NO, what do we need to do to earn a higher rating?_____
   _____
   _____
   _____

6. If you have an e-mail address, *or need to update your current address*, please indicate below:
   E-mail Address: _____

7. How satisfied are you with the management of your portfolio and overall advice? _____
   _____
   _____

8. What do you think differentiates [Insert Company Name] from other wealth-planning firms with which you have worked? _____
   _____

FIGURE 8.3 *Prospect and Referrals (Used when a prospect asks for information about our firm), continued*

---

9. Referrals are the primary way that [Insert Company Name] grows. Whom do you know who would benefit from receiving information about our firm?

Name: _____   Phone: _____
Address: _____

Calculate the Customer Service Index (CSI) by totaling the responses given for Question #4. Also, if the client indicates "Yes" on Question #5, give yourself one extra point. To get the final calculation, add the total responses from Question #4 plus the extra points generated from Question #5 and divide the overall score by the number of surveys received back for that month.

Example:

Scores for Question #4 over a one-month period	10	9	9	9	10
Additional Score if Question #5 is a Yes	1	1	0	1	1
Total:	11	10	9	10	11

Divide the grand total by the number of surveys returned: $51 \div 5 = 10.2$

The original survey is given to the Office Manager to review. Any survey returned with a rating of 8 or below on question #4 receives a phone call to determine where the problem lies.

At the end of each quarter, place all the returned surveys in a hat and draw a winner. Send the winner a small gift such as a gift certificate or a box of steaks.

Updates
Update Notebooks

Each advisor keeps an alphabetized set of notebooks containing the advisor's clients' updates in his or her office. When a client calls with questions or requesting money, the advisor has easy access to the client's entire portfolio without pulling the file.

1. A consolidated report is completed at least three days prior to the advisor's meeting with the client or when requested by the client or advisor for mailing.

2. After a meeting with a client, advisors will give the update to the New Business Coordinator (transfers), the Trading Manager (buys or sells), or the Portfolio Update Manager (file in the update book/ make corrections). Transfers and/or buys and sells need to be done immediately. Then the update is given to the Portfolio Update Manager for filing.

(continued)

FIGURE 8.3 *Prospect and Referrals (Used when a prospect asks for information about our firm), continued*

3. The update is three-hole punched and alphabetized in the book after transfers and/or buys and sells are made.

4. The old update is pulled out of the update notebooks and filed in the client file.

5. On an as-needed basis, the books should be checked against the client list to be certain all the updates are in the notebooks.

6. Enter the date and type of update in the Contact Management System.

7. TRANSFERRING CLIENTS—When a client transfers his or her account out of your firm, the update should be pulled out of the book and filed in the client file.

8. DECEASED CLIENTS—When a client dies, the update should be left in the book if the beneficiary will be leaving the portfolio with your firm. If the beneficiary is moving the portfolio out, the update should stay in the update notebook until the transfers are complete.

Client Appreciation
Client Events—Supplies

Use the following checklist to ensure the appropriate supplies are available for each client event. All supplies are kept in a covered tub in the literature room. The box needs to be checked before each workshop.

_____ 1. Name tags—client and prospect

_____ 2. Two to three blank sheets of name tags (blue border) per rep—clients
   Two blank sheets of name tags (no border)—prospects

_____ 3. One thick marking pen for name tags

_____ 4. One pen and notepad for notes; Post-it notes

_____ 5. Paper clips; Scotch tape

_____ 6. Extra light bulb if our slide projector is being used

_____ 7. Five to ten prospect packets

_____ 8. Two sign-in sheets for guests

_____ 9. Any materials the speaker shipped to us ahead of time for distribution

FIGURE 8.3 *Prospect and Referrals (Used when a prospect asks for information about our firm), continued*

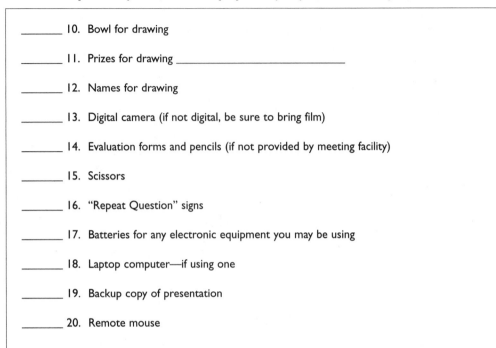

_____ 10. Bowl for drawing

_____ 11. Prizes for drawing _____

_____ 12. Names for drawing

_____ 13. Digital camera (if not digital, be sure to bring film)

_____ 14. Evaluation forms and pencils (if not provided by meeting facility)

_____ 15. Scissors

_____ 16. "Repeat Question" signs

_____ 17. Batteries for any electronic equipment you may be using

_____ 18. Laptop computer—if using one

_____ 19. Backup copy of presentation

_____ 20. Remote mouse

Office Procedures

The Six Most Important Things to Do Tomorrow

Each afternoon before leaving work, make a list of the six most important things you need to do the next business day. The list must be in order of priority and must be placed on top of your desk at the end of the day.

At the end of each day, determine if you took a step forward or a step backward.

There are several advantages to creating this list every day.

1. If you are ill, another team member can quickly identify your priority items that must be addressed while you are out.

2. The list provides a starting point for you each day. You will not waste time trying to decide what to work on first. In addition, once you have made the list, you will spend less time worrying about work-related activities during the evening or weekend.

(continued)

FIGURE 8.3 *Prospect and Referrals (Used when a prospect asks for information about our firm), continued*

3. Even though you will have many interruptions during the day, when you return to the list, you will always be working on the most important items.

4. After making the list for 30 days, you will find that it has become a habit.

6 MOST

Date:

1.	
2.	
3.	
4.	
5.	
6.	

Other To-Do Activities

Current Projects	Longer-term Projects

Human Resources

Team Member Leaving Early System

If you have an emergency and have to leave early, please do the following:

1. Talk to your supervisor and explain the situation.

FIGURE 8.3 *Prospect and Referrals (Used when a prospect asks for information about our firm), continued*

---

2. Change your voice mail—example: "Hello, this is **[Insert Your Name]**, with **[Insert Company Name]**. Today is **[Insert Date]**. I will be out of the office for the remainder of the day. If you need to speak to someone right away, please dial 0 and the receptionist will redirect your call to an available team member. If this is not a time-sensitive matter, please leave your name and number, and I will return your call as soon as possible. Thanks and have a great day."

3. Put your phone on "Do not disturb."

4. Let the receptionist know that you will be out of the office for the rest of the day.

5. If you have any urgent work/appointments that need to be done that day, give them to your immediate supervisor.

If possible, check your voice mail periodically throughout the day. For example, if you leave at 11:00 a.m., check it around 1:00 and again before the end of the day.

SUMMARY

- Having a system allows you to deliver a high level of service on a consistent basis.
- A system is a formalized mechanism that helps ensure you perform an activity according to a certain standard.
- The nine areas to systematize are Prospects and Referrals, New Clients, Transfers, Trading, Client Service, Updates, Client Appreciation, Office Procedures, and Human Resources.
- Creating and using your own Systems Manual is critical to building a world-class financial services business.
- Creating and using systems provide you with three main benefits. First, it increases your efficiency, which leads to an improved quality of life. Second, your office will commit fewer errors. And third, it helps new staff members get up to speed faster.

TNT #3 ACTION STEPS

- Make systematizing your office one of your goals for this year.

- Identify the key staff person who will have overall responsibility for systematizing your office.

- Add systematizing your office to your results-based pay compensation system.

- Systematize your office in the following order:
    1. Prospects and Referrals
    2. New Clients
    3. Transfers
    4. Trading
    5. Client Service
    6. Updates
    7. Client Appreciation
    8. Office Procedures
    9. Human Resources

- Review your systems on a periodic basis to make sure they are still effective.

IMPROVE YOUR
EFFECTIVENESS

9

DIFFERENTIATE BETWEEN THE VITAL FEW AND THE TRIVIAL MANY

"It is those who make the worst use of their time who most complain of its shortness."
—JEAN DE LA BRUYERE

Nineteenth-century economist Vilfredo Pareto made an extremely useful observation around the dawn of the 20th century. He observed that in most societies wealth was unequally distributed. Specifically, he noticed that about 20 percent of the top earners in society accounted for about 80 percent of the wealth. Of course, we know this today as the 80/20 rule.

In the 1930s and 1940s, Dr. J. M. Juran, a quality improvement researcher, discovered that the 80/20 principle was applicable not just in wealth distribution but in universal laws too. Juran called it the "vital few and the trivial many." The name didn't stick but the concept did.

The "vital few and trivial many" concept should become a mantra for all advisors. Unfortunately, for many advisors the emphasis is on the "trivial many," and that's one reason why they're not able to break through production plateaus.

In our industry, we have $100,000 producers, $5 million producers, and everything in between. Where you fall in that range has a lot to do with how you spend your time.

Imagine there's a table in front of you with a large glass jar, a scoop of pebbles, a water bottle, several rocks, and a handful of sand. If your goal were to fill the jar with each of those items, in what order would you fill it?

The most efficient way would be to put the rocks in first, followed by the pebbles, sand, and water. Top producers know this intuitively. They take care of the rocks first—that is, the high-impact activities for which they are singularly qualified. The remaining items—pebbles, sand, water—are simply "stuff" that they either delegate or eliminate.

It's not about working harder or smarter or more efficiently. Top producers work more *effectively*. Working effectively means you're doing the right things the right way. It means you're focused on the "vital few" and are completing those activities the right way.

The only way to determine your effectiveness is to measure it, and that means tracking your time. We've developed a Time Management Tracking Sheet to make this easy for you. Simply go to http://www.peakproductions.com/timetracking and download it. Use this sheet to track your time for two weeks and then add up the numbers.

For comparison purposes, below are the top ten stones for a typical million-dollar producer (are your stones the same?):

1. **Reviewing client goals and objectives, managing assets, and conducting research.** As a financial professional, these are some of your primary tasks.
2. **Communicating with A+ clients.** Your top clients want to stay informed. You can do that via the phone, e-mail, regular mail, or meeting with them in person.
3. **Taking care of fitness.** Yes, for many top producers fitness is a rock. By staying healthy, you'll have the stamina and the energy you need to face each day with enthusiasm and confidence.

4. **Sharpening the saw.** Spending time on continuing education, new laws and strategies, and reviewing new products pays dividends.
5. **Cultivating A+ referrals.** Great service is not enough. You have to let your clients know you want referrals; train them to spot referral opportunities, and make sending referrals part of your compensation.
6. **Deepening A+ and A relationships.** You don't have to be all business. Spend time with your clients in nonbusiness settings such as taking them out to lunch, playing a round of golf, or hosting a wine-tasting event.
7. **Developing centers of influence.** A handful of centers of influence can make a dramatic impact on your business. Look beyond the obvious ones (CPAs, attorneys) and be creative. Try the head of your chamber of commerce or one of your town's leading philanthropists.
8. **Planning.** By spending time planning your day, week, and month, you'll stay focused and productive.
9. **Delivering A+ and A client solutions.** Explaining your recommendations, hand holding, and responding to questions are all important parts of building enduring relationships.
10. **Meeting with staff.** Regularly scheduled staff meetings will help reduce interruptions and increase your efficiency.

If you're like the other advisors who completed this time survey, you probably found some shocking results. Here's what we found.

Top producers spend about 75 percent of their time on these top ten activities. Notice that the activities are concentrated on the A+ and A clients. These are the clients who will help you take your practice to the next level. By focusing your attention on them, you can deepen your relationship, improve your service, and generate more referrals.

Conversely, top producers spend 0 percent of their time dealing with B, C, and D clients and prospects, and average producers spend 22 percent of their time here. Imagine what would happen to your practice if you could devote an extra two hours per day to working with your A+ and A clients without adding to the total hours you work? Do you think your production would increase and your quality of life improve? Of course they would. One of the keys to unlocking these extra two hours in your office is to hire an Associate Wealth Advisor as we discussed in TNT #2.

So how do you go about becoming more effective by focusing on the "vital few" activities and eliminating the "trivial many"? It's a process, so let's begin.

Step 1. Admit that you have a problem. Advisors who get caught up in the "trivial many" have a problem distinguishing between perception and reality. Much as we said in TNT #2 about when to hire staff, your perception may be one of the following:

- You're the only one who can do a certain activity.
- It's easier for you to do it than to train somebody else.
- It only takes a minute, so it's not worth letting somebody else do it.

The reality is just the opposite.

- Somebody else can usually do certain activities better than you.
- Spending training time on the front end will save much more time on the back end.
- Fifteen minutes a day of activities that "only take a few minutes to do" add up to one and a half weeks per year. Just imagine what you could do with an extra one and a half weeks per year.

As you let your staff take over some of your activities, they may make some mistakes and that's okay. Just grit your teeth, exhibit leadership, and they'll learn from the experience and do better the next time. The sooner you get over the idea that you have to do everything, the sooner you'll be on your way to a better quality of life.

Step 2. Identify the "vital few" activities for your practice. Think for a moment: If you could do only three activities for the rest of your career, what would they be? What three activities would have the highest impact on your business? Based on our experience and the results from our time survey with million-dollar producers, the three key activities you should spend the bulk of your time on are generating A+ and A clients, meeting with A+ and A clients, and planning for A+ and A clients. Those are the three key things you are uniquely qualified to do, and they should consume about 75 percent of your time.

Now, in order to do those three things, you need to spend some time preparing and educating yourself. This means you'll also have to spend some time sharpening the saw, staying fit, planning and engaging in personal reflection, and meeting with your staff. These activities should take about 25 percent of your time.

Step 3. Learn to delegate. Delegating requires that you change your attitude from "I'm the only one who can do this" to a new attitude of "I can train somebody else to do this." A key thing to remember is, you don't want your staff to push back at you and say, "I feel as if I'm being dumped on." As you delegate, do it in a caring, respectful way.

How do you decide what to delegate? You should delegate everything in your office that another staff member has the ability to do and can do for less than your hourly compensation. If it's a job or task that no other staff member can presently do, ask yourself, Can I train a staff member to do it, or can I hire some-one else to do it?

Here are a few other key ideas to remember when you delegate:

- Be clear about the job you are delegating and the results or outcome that you expect.
- Give your staff members some latitude in how they complete the job. If they are able to use some of their own creativity, they will be more excited about doing it.
- Expect your staff to finish the job rather than take it only to a certain level and then pass it back to you for completion. Invest more time in training them if necessary so they can complete the job.

Delegation is about empowerment. You're empowering your staff to increase their responsibility within your firm; when you have the right staff members, they accept it willingly.

Step 4. Delegate but don't abdicate. The goal of delegation is to free you to focus on your higher value activities and to empower your staff. This doesn't mean you can just push off your activities to another staff member and forget about it. You still need to train your staff member in the activity you're delegating, be available for questions, and follow up periodically to make sure it's going well. As time goes on, your staff member will become proficient at the activity and your involvement will be minimal.

Invest time on the front end and you'll save time on the back end.

PERSONAL EFFECTIVENESS TIPS

It's easy for slippage to occur throughout your day, whether it's staff interruptions, client calls, Websurfing, or just plain lack of motivation. But if you want to grow, you've got to replace the slippage with a renewed focus on your key activities. Here are a few ideas that will help.

"The Six Most Important"

Ron is a huge proponent of this simple idea that helps you stay focused during the day. Here's Ron describing the genesis of the idea:

> About 75 years ago, steel magnate Charles Schwab, the first president of U.S. Steel and the founder of Bethlehem Steel (no relation to brokerage king Charles Schwab), came in contact with Ivy Lee, a consultant who went on to cofound one of the country's first public relations firms. Schwab was looking for a way to become more efficient, and Lee had just the solution. As the story goes, Lee told Schwab his idea and then told Schwab to follow it religiously for 30 days. Lee was so confident in his idea that he told Schwab to withhold payment for the idea until after those 30 days, and at that time Schwab could pay him whatever he thought the idea was worth.
>
> Being an overachiever, Schwab followed the idea and by the end of 30 days was blown away by the results. Pleased with the success, Schwab handed Lee a check for $25,000, a significant sum in those days. So what was this big idea?
>
> *Every evening before you leave work, write down the six most important activities you have to accomplish the next day in order of priority and leave the list on your desk. Begin the next day working on item #1 and work your way sequentially through the list, making sure you do not move on to the next item until the current item is completed.*
>
> It's a deceptively simple concept to understand, yet it's frustratingly difficult for people to implement. The end-of-the-day rush gets in the way, you're late for dinner, the kids have

a ball game—you know the drill. It's easy to let it slip. But with a little better planning, this idea will become a ritual that happens as effortlessly as tying your shoes. We've been writing down our six most important activities to accomplish the next day every day for years, as has our staff. The bottom line: it works for us, it works for our coaching clients, and it will work for you and your staff, too.

If you have trouble getting your staff to do it consistently, here's a quick remedy: make it part of their results-based pay bonus. Remember, 60 percent of their quarterly bonus should be based on individual goals, and one of those individual goals can be writing down the six most important every day. Ask your staff to put the list on their desk before they leave for the day. Occasionally, you can walk by and spot check if they've done it. One of our coaching clients became quite creative in terms of motivating her staff to write down the "six most important." She went on vacation for two weeks and on her return asked to see each team member's "six most" sheets. Then the surprise came. For each sheet the team member turned in, he or she got a crisp $10 bill. Those who had no sheets had pretty long faces from missing out on some cold, hard cash.

Prioritizing your "six most important" list is critical. Begin your day by working on the number one item. You may end up spending your whole day working on that item and, if so, should take comfort in knowing that you were focused on the single most important activity for that day. If you are between meetings or find you have a few extra minutes, scan your list and try to find an item that will take about as long to accomplish as you have time available. This may take you out of order, but you'll still be working on one of the day's most important activities and are able to efficiently fill up your time. Your total list may be longer than six items; that's fine, but keep the top six prominent and prioritized.

By spending these few minutes each day before you leave the office, your subconscious mind will absorb the list overnight, and you'll start the next day focused and ready to tackle the day's activities.

The Mission and Vision

Earlier, we asked you to develop a personal and professional mission statement and a vision statement. These documents give you clarity of purpose and direction, and with that you find it becomes much easier to decide what's important and where you should spend your time. Your mission and vision effectively become a "not-to-do" list. So the next time you're contemplating an activity, ask yourself, Is this activity moving me closer to achieving my mission and vision? If the answer is no, then don't do it or delegate it to somebody else.

Streamline Your Product List

Focus on a handful of products that you can efficiently monitor and thoroughly understand. Some advisors we've worked with had literally hundreds of different securities spread across their clients' portfolios. Trying to monitor and understand that many investments is next to impossible. Instead, develop your own approved list, create several model portfolios, and then try to slot your clients into them. You'll end up with a short list of securities to monitor, and when you need to make a change, it will be much easier to do.

Clean Your Office and Clear Your Desk

It's draining to walk into an office that's filled with papers, books, files, and literature. On the other hand, walking into an office that's clean with an uncluttered desk sends a clear message to your brain that you're organized and ready to tackle the day's opportunities. It's subtle but effective.

Become a Planner

Planning is especially important when it comes to reducing your daily slippage. By knowing what you're going to do throughout the day, you'll eliminate dead time and be more productive. The key is to use some type of calendar system, so if you're not using one, get one. Which type of calendar system you use is not as important as the fact that you use one. In our office, we use a customized version of GoldMine® that we modified specifically for a financial-planning practice. The calendar function is excellent and lets each of our staff members maintain his or her own calendar as well as view each other's. This system is available to other advisors, so if you want to learn more, please visit http://www .peakproductions.com.

All of our activities, appointments, phone calls, and the like are scheduled on the calendar. When we're in the office, the system is loaded, so we can easily look at it or see an alert pop-up. When we're traveling, we simply print the calendar and take a paper copy along or log in remotely through the Internet and access it as if we were sitting in our office.

There's one principle we want you to always keep in mind: keep it simple. If you get a sophisticated PDA that keeps you connected 24/7, you'll probably end up spending more time hassling with the system than the time you're saving. In the end, the most effective planning system is the one that gets used.

When it comes to planning, here are four keys to keep in mind.

1. **Use time blocking.** When you have an important activity to do, block time on your calendar to do it. For example, if

you're writing a book, block time on your calendar. If you're working on goals for the New Year, block time on your calendar. If your child has a ball game or a recital, block that time on your calendar. If you're going to be out of town, block that on your calendar too. In fact, it's helpful to block out at least half a day before you leave and half a day after you return. That way, you won't be stressed before you leave or get depressed when you return and have to jump right back into appointments. You shouldn't be interrupted during your time block unless it's an emergency.

2. **Schedule your high-value activities in bunches.** Athletes get in the "zone," financial advisors get in the "groove." Athletes practice, practice, practice, and then they are called on to perform. It's no different for you. You prepare, prepare, prepare, and then you are called on to perform. But unlike athletes, your "season" is year-round, so you have no extended recuperating phase. The best way around that is to bunch your high-value activities into one, two, or three days each week. That way you can muster your energy and prepare yourself psychologically to give your maximum effort on certain days and have some rest periods in between.

But remember—stress will kill you. Even in your "bunch days," you have to have some breaks. For every 90 to 120 minutes that you're "performing," take a 15- to 20-minute break to decompress, eat a healthy snack, and regain your energy level.

3. **Schedule your activities as far in advance as possible.** As soon as you know something is planned, get it on your calendar even if it's tentative. If you're in a coaching program, schedule time to work on the material, attend the meetings, and participate in the phone calls. Schedule your vacation time. The more you can plan in advance, the more productive you'll be and the less chance you'll run into a double scheduling problem.

4. **Know your prime time.** Some people function best early in the morning, others later in the day. Determine your prime time and try to schedule your highest value activities during that time.

Use a Dictation Service

We can speak much faster than we can write or type, so we signed up for a telephone-based dictation service, which allows us to dial a phone number and leave our voice message. A short time later we receive an e-mail with our transcribed voice message. We can then "cut and paste" this text into a letter or into the history section of our contact management system. We can even forward the e-mail to somebody else. It's a very efficient way to complete a written message, and because it's easier than typing, we tend to have more detailed and descriptive messages for our records and letters. As an advisor, it's a great compliance tool because we can create detailed notes on client conversations and meetings and store them in our contact management system. To receive a discount on this service and other favorite vendors that we use, visit http://www.peakproductions.com and click on the favorite vendors link. That will contain the most up-to-date list of the vendors we've had good success with.

Consider Voice Mail instead of E-mail for Your Intracompany Communication

Most companies have a distinct culture of either voice mail or e-mail. We've found voice mail to be more convenient because you can easily leave a detailed message, and all you need is a phone to retrieve it. It allows you to work from the golf course or the beach if necessary.

SUMMARY

- As an entrepreneur, time flexibility is one of your luxuries . . . but it's also a curse. It's very easy to get distracted and let slippage creep into your day. If you follow the ideas we've outlined here, your days will be more productive and your business more profitable.

- It's not about working harder or smarter or more efficiently. Top producers work more *effectively*. Working effectively means you're doing the right things the right way. It means you're focused on the "vital few" and you're completing those activities the right way.

- Every evening before you leave work, write down the six most important activities you have to accomplish the next day in order of priority and leave the list on your desk. Begin the next day working on item #1 and work your way sequentially through the list making sure you do not move on to the next item until the current item is completed.

- Focus on a handful of products that you can efficiently monitor and thoroughly understand.

- Use time blocking.

- Schedule your high-value activities in bunches.

- Schedule your activities as far in advance as possible.

- Know your prime time.

- Use a dictation service.

10

GET AND STAY FIT

"The first wealth is health."
—RALPH WALDO EMERSON

You probably didn't expect to find information on health and fitness in a financial advisor practice management book, did you? Well, health and fitness permeate everything we do, and if there's slippage in your health, there will be slippage in your business. There's no sense working hard to build your business and then be in such poor health that you can't enjoy the fruits of your labor.

We've included health and fitness here in the productivity section because all the things we discuss in this book have one thing in common—they all require energy to accomplish. If you're yawning and dragging during the day, there's no way you can be productive and operate at full capacity.

Think for a moment about someone you know who always exudes energy and enthusiasm. Then think about someone you know who seems lethargic and uninspired. Who is more successful? Who would you rather be around? Your clients are no different. They want to be around people who radiate energy and are filled with enthusiasm.

Energy comes from two sources. First, you get energy by connecting with your values and doing the things that bring you excitement, enthusiasm, and satisfaction. Ever notice when you're engaged in an activity you really enjoy or are surrounded by the people you love that you have boundless energy? It's an effortless state that makes time fly by. The opposite is also true. When you're engaged in activities you don't enjoy, your energy level goes down and you start to drag.

This is one of the many reasons why the Blueprinting exercises are so important. You can't connect with your deepest values if you don't know what they are.

Second, you get energy from the physical side. According to authors Jim Loehr and Tony Schwartz in their book *The Power of Full Engagement* (Free Press, 2003), physical energy comes from the interaction of a variety of factors, such as the foods you eat, your pattern of breathing, the quality and quantity of your sleep, your degree of periodic recovery, and your overall level of fitness.

Staying fit and keeping your energy level high are important components of being successful not just as an advisor but, more important, as a human being. Here are some ideas to consider, but before you begin, make sure you talk to your doctor and get the doctor's advice on dos and don'ts that are specific for your level of fitness.

Hire a Personal Trainer

Rather than become an expert yourself, hire one. The quickest way to get started on an exercise program is to join a gym and hire a qualified personal trainer. A trainer can work closely with you to develop an exercise and nutrition plan that is specific to you and meets the goals you have set. In addition, paying for your sessions and having someone take a personal interest in your success increase your odds of sticking to the plan.

Focus on Losing Body Fat, Not Lean Body Mass

Your body consists of fat and lean body mass. Lean body mass is everything else but fat and includes muscle, bones, skin, water, organs, blood, and hair. Working toward an appropriate level of body fat should be one of your fitness goals. Body fat measurements are typically done with calipers, which are used to measure skin folds at various points on your body. The calipers yield a body fat percentage that is simply the number of pounds of your fat divided by your total body weight.

According to the American Council on Exercise, the appropriate body fat for women is in the low to mid-20 percent range. For men, the appropriate range is in the middle to upper teens. By comparison, athletes typically have body fat below 10 percent.

As you start your exercise program, get your body fat measured. Most gyms provide that service. Then consult with your trainer and determine an appropriate body fat goal. The trick is to lose body fat but not lose lean body mass. You don't want to get thinner *and weaker* at the same time. Combining aerobic exercise with strength training and a proper diet will help you move toward the appropriate balance between body fat and lean body mass.

Maintaining an appropriate percent of body fat has numerous health benefits. You'll reduce your risk of heart disease, high blood pressure, osteoarthritis, and various other ailments. In addition, the more muscle you have, the more calories you'll burn each day. This means you can actually eat more food with a lower percent of body fat and not gain weight compared with someone who weighs the same as you but has a higher percent of body fat.

Do Aerobic Exercise

Do you get winded going up a flight of stairs? Does walking around the block or hiking up a hill tax you? If so, your cardiovascular system needs some work. When minor exertion causes you to breathe rapidly, it means your heart has to work harder to pump blood through your system. Aerobic exercise strengthens your heart and allows it to pump more blood with each beat. The more blood it can pump with each beat, the more work you can accomplish without getting out of breath.

Improving your cardiovascular system can be as easy as taking a brisk 30- to 45-minute walk four to six times a week. If you're more aggressive, work up to a 30-minute jog three to four days a week. Even if you live in a cold climate, don't let the weather stop you. Dressed appropriately (layers, synthetic fabrics, wind jacket, and pants), a 30-minute walk in ten below zero weather with snow on the ground can be not only healthy for you but also pleasant and invigorating. Hey, don't laugh, we're from Nebraska, so we have to make it sound good!

Other great forms of aerobic exercise include biking, swimming, and hiking. To keep it interesting, mix it up. Adding a little variety keeps you on track longer and makes the experience more enjoyable.

Aerobic exercise not only helps build a stronger heart but has other benefits too. Of course, you burn calories so it helps you lose weight. It can also make you happier. Exercise helps release endorphins, which are chemicals from the brain that have been linked to feelings of euphoria and reduced stress and anxiety. Your immune system also benefits from aerobic exercise as you'll become less susceptible to minor colds and the flu.

Lift Weights

Aerobic exercise alone won't cut it. Even though it will improve your cardiovascular system, which is great, you could end up trim but weak. After about age 35, we lose roughly half a pound of muscle a year. Consequently, if you don't do strength training, you'll start adding more fat and become weaker and more susceptible to osteoporosis.

Hitting the weights two to three days a week for 30 to 60 minutes is a great way to keep your muscles active and growing. Follow your trainer's advice, make sure you get adequate rest in between, and you'll see results reasonably soon.

Watch Your Diet

Doing aerobic exercise and lifting weights are two-thirds of the puzzle. The other third is eating properly. There's certainly no lack of diet books to choose from, although most of them are worthless. Any diet that significantly deviates from a normal, well-balanced plan is a recipe for failure. If you have to rely on willpower to sustain the diet, you'll eventually fail.

We think the best diet is a common-sense one that focuses on eating five to six small, well-balanced meals a day. Eat lots of lean protein (e.g., egg whites), complex carbohydrates (e.g., green vegetables), and "good" fats (e.g., raw almonds and flax seeds). Two major things to watch out for are unnecessary sugar and salt. You'll get plenty of sugar in your fruit, so don't compound it by adding sugar to your cereal or oatmeal. And if you have pie, pizza, or ice cream occasionally, don't stress out over it. Follow the 80/20 rule—eat well 80 percent of the time and don't feel guilty indulging the other 20 percent. The key is to develop a nutrition plan that consists of foods you like and that are good for you. If you develop a nutrition plan that you can sustain because you eat the foods you like in appropriate portions, then you'll never have to be on a "diet."

Consider supplements too, such as protein shakes and protein bars. The bars in particular are convenient when you're traveling. Nuts are another convenient source of good food while you're traveling.

Get Quality Sleep

If we're fortunate, we'll have at least 30,000 days on this earth to make our mark on society. Of those, roughly 10,000 will be spent sleeping, 10,000 will be spent working, and 10,000 will be spent getting ready for work, eating, socializing, and running errands.

Imagine that: one-third of our life is spent sleeping, yet most of us pay little attention to it. When something has to "give" during the day, frequently it's our sleep. That's unfortunate because sleeping can be an extremely restorative, rejuvenating, and energizing activity that makes our 20,000 waking days healthier and more productive. Proper sleep habits go a long way toward helping you become and remain a peak performer.

How can you tell if you're not getting the proper amount of sleep? According to James Maas, author of *Power Sleep,* you're not getting the proper amount of sleep if you experience any of the following:

- Daytime drowsiness
- Mood shifts, including depression, increased irritability, and loss of sense of humor
- Stress, anxiety, and loss of coping skills
- Lack of interest in socializing with others
- Weight gain
- Feelings of being chilled
- Reduced immunity to disease and viral infection
- Feelings of lethargy
- Reduced productivity

Volatile markets have no doubt caused part of our sleep problem. The stress from clients can be very draining indeed and affect the quality of our sleep. Yet there are some basic steps we can take to reduce this stress and significantly improve our night's rest. Here are eight tips:

1. Ideally, you should go to bed at the same time every night. However, that's not always practical. So if you have to go to bed late, get up at your regular time in the morning and then try to take a nap the next day or go to bed earlier that night.

2. Although it's tempting, don't sleep later on the weekends. You'll pay for it on Monday!

3. Exercise regularly and eat five to six light meals a day that are balanced in carbohydrates, protein, and fat. And don't forget your fruits and vegetables (especially your green vegetables as they're rich in antioxidants and low in sugar).

4. Create a bedtime ritual such as reading a book for a few minutes before you turn the lights out. It signals your body that it's time for bed.

5. Consciously relax your mind at bedtime. Let go of those stressful thoughts and focus your mind on relaxation, positive imagery, and deep breathing.

6. If you can't fall asleep after 30 minutes, don't just lie there tossing and turning. Get up, read a book, and then go back to bed when you start feeling sleepy.

7. If you wake up during the night feeling alive and refreshed, congratulations! Get up and start your day—your body is telling you you've had enough rest for that night.

8. Keep your sleeping environment dark and cool—about 65° is the ideal temperature.

By spending time improving your sleeping hours, you'll make your waking hours healthier and more productive.

By making the effort to improve your health, the dividends are much greater than just physical. And remember, nothing tastes as great as being healthy feels.

SUMMARY

This short chapter on health and fitness is obviously not a comprehensive guide to getting and staying fit. Our objective in including it is to simply highlight its importance to your quality of life and to pique your interest in learning more. There are some excellent resources available to you including:

- *Body for Life* (HarperCollins, 1999) by Bill Phillips (an excellent beginners guide to diet and weight training)
- *Power Sleep* by James Maas (some great information on improving the quality of your sleep)
- http://www.mayoclinic.com (an outstanding source for health and nutrition information)

TNT #4 ACTION STEPS

- Go to http://www.peakproductions.com/timetracking and download the time-tracking spreadsheet. Use this sheet to track your time for two weeks and then add up the numbers. Compare your results with the results of million-dollar producers shown in Chapter 9.

- Follow the four-step process to get focused on the "vital few" activities in your office.

- Start writing down your "six most important" every day.

- Streamline your product list.

- Start time blocking.

- Start using a dictation service. Visit the Peak Productions Web site at http://www.peakproductions.com, click on the favorite vendors link, and sign up for the recommended dictation service.

- Hire a personal trainer and get fit!

- Follow the 80/20 rule when it comes to eating.

- Get quality sleep.

BUILD YOUR BRAND

11

MOVE YOUR BUSINESS FROM COMMODITY TO SINGULARITY

"They're not the best at what they do; they're the only ones who do what they do."

—BILL GRAHAM commenting on The Grateful Dead

Financial services is a commodity business. Technically, you're competing with roughly 500,000 active registered representatives, 42,000 Certified Financial Planners™, 180,000 insurance professionals, plus countless investment advisors. All these people pretty much sell the same products, use similar technology platforms, and follow generally accepted principles of financial management. In that environment, it's tough to get an edge . . . unless you build a distinctive brand.

By building your brand, you'll end up with zero competitors. Your firm will become singularly qualified to handle the complex financial needs of your target clientele. The key is to realize that you can't be all things to all people, but you can be all things to a small group of carefully chosen people who value your advice, service, and relationship. And it doesn't take a large number of clients to be financially successful in this business. According to studies by anthropologist Robin Dunbar, humans are capable of having meaningful interaction with about 150 people. Get much above that and we lose our ability to make a connection. With an average account size of $667,000 and a 1 percent average annual fee, 150 clients will generate $1 million in annual revenue—a financial success by industry standards.

Branding can help you get those 150 key relationships.

HOW DO YOU BUILD YOUR BRAND?

Everybody reading this book has a brand, but it may not be the brand that you want. So what is your brand? It's real simple to find out. Just ask five of your clients this question:

"Mr. and Mrs. Jones, when you hear the name of my firm, what do you think of?"

If they give you that deer-in-the-headlights look, then you know you've got a problem. On the other hand, they may say:

> When I think of your firm, I think of a company that's always looking out for my best interest, that makes me feel like I'm part of a family, and that I would trust to handle my mother's money, and in fact, you do handle my mother's account. Your service is impeccable, you're proactive, and you give me financial peace of mind.

When you get that kind of response, you know you've developed an unassailable brand that will make you stand out in a commodity business. So how do you build this unassailable brand? Think of the acronym VIPER™.

V stands for Vision, Values, and Value

A clear vision for your business rooted in core values is a great foundation for delivering value to your clients.

Vision. Great brands are backed by an inspiring vision that engenders loyalty, passion, and emotional involvement among your staff members and your clients. A vision is a compelling picture of your perfect business. It's what you're striving toward. Can you imagine trying to build a strong brand when your staff members aren't clear about your company's vision? You can't. And if your staff isn't clear about your vision, there's no way your clients will be either. That's why having a vision and having a staff that's well-connected to that vision is so critical.

Remember the movie *The Blues Brothers?* Elwood Blues says, "We're on a mission from God." That's the level of passion and enthusiasm you should strive to ignite in your staff members. When they feel that passion and connection, it becomes contagious with all the people they come in contact with. When your clients get wind of it, they can't help but become enamored with your firm and become clients for life.

Values. Great brands stand for something. They have an enduring core that transcends bull and bear markets. Your business's core values are like the lighthouse in the storm that guides you to the shore. They're your rock, they give you stability, and they help you make the right decisions in difficult circumstances.

One of the biggest mistakes of advisors when defining their values is making them too fluffy. Generic values such as "the best service" or "quality advice" are plastered all over advisors' marketing material. Unfortunately, when prospects read that stuff, their eyes glaze over. People are conditioned to discount broad claims because they have no basis for making a comparison. Instead, really analyze what is central to your company's existence. What have you done so well that has attracted people to your firm? Why do your clients keep doing business with you instead of moving to someone else? What have you done consistently well over the years through good and bad markets?

You should be able to come up with a list of values that help set your firm apart from the rest. Once you have this list, put on your wordsmith hat and figure out how to eloquently and definitively describe your core values. Make sure you get rid of the fluff and write something that is 100 percent you. It should reflect what you've been delivering for years in your business.

For example, Yahoo! has a list of six core values: excellence, innovation, customer fixation, teamwork, community, and fun. This last core value in particular is definitely 100 percent Yahoo! The company describes its "fun" core value by saying, "We believe humor is essential to success. We applaud irreverence and don't take ourselves too seriously. We celebrate achievement. We yodel."

Just by its name you can tell Yahoo! is a fun company, and it's done a great job incorporating that value throughout the company. Even though fun may not be one of your core values, the idea is to find what's special about you and live by it.

By homing in on a core set of values, you can incorporate those values into everything you do in your business. For example, you can integrate your values into your printed marketing material, your Web site and even your conversations with your clients and prospects. By letting your clients and prospects know who you are and what you stand for, you'll deepen your relationship and enhance your brand.

Value. Great brands promise and deliver value. What value do you bring to your client relationships that they can't get somewhere else? It's not the products or services you offer. It's not your stock-picking skill. It's simply you and everything you stand for and deliver. Ultimately, prospects look you in the eye and say to themselves, Do I trust that this person will always be a good steward of my money, will always be looking out for my best interests, and will always be a valued partner in my financial situation?

Delivering value is multidimensional. It encompasses a variety of areas such as service, results relative to expectations, trustworthiness, and caring. It involves figuring out how to make your clients' life easier and less stressful. True value providers know their clients better than their clients know themselves. More specifically, you should know your clients well enough to be contacting them about things they should be doing well before they even know they have a need. For example, prior to the invention of the SONY Walkman, nobody knew they had a need for a portable tape player with headphones. But SONY knew its clients so well that it developed the product, created a new market, and made millions.

We operate in such a competitive business that if somebody comes up with a great value-adding idea, it is quickly cloned. The real trick is not just to add value but to create *sustainable* value. So how do you create sustainable value? The answer is to deliver to other people what will always be scarce.

People always pay for what is always in short supply. And what is always in short supply? There are three things: time, wisdom, and trust.

Time. As Jim Croce so poignantly sang back in 1975, ". . . there never seems to be enough time to do the things you want to do, once you find them." But the fact is, we've always had 24 hours in a day and that's never going to change—yet every year there are more and more things that compete for our time. For example, in the early 1990s, nobody was on the Internet. Today, of course, you've got to allot half your day just to answering your e-mail.

You can create sustainable value by helping your clients save time. You want them to feel that you have figured out how to make their life easier and less stressful. Handle the financial aspect of their life, so they don't have to spend hours worrying about it. You not only save them time in planning and meeting their financial goals, but you also enable them to have the cash on hand to do the things they want to do in that extra time.

Wisdom. We are bombarded by information, yet information alone does not equal wisdom. On the contrary, clients can feel inundated and confused by the barrage of information that hits them daily.

The Internet is filled with billions and billions of pages of information that's a jumbled mass of fact, fiction, and everything in between. Yet companies like Yahoo! and Google built multibillion-dollar organizations by simply categorizing and indexing a portion of that information. Imagine what those companies would be worth if they found a way to convert the Internet's information into true wisdom!

As an advisor, you have the power to spin some of that straw into gold with your expertise. You want your clients to think of you as the person who makes sense of it all, the person who understands and uses all that financial information to recommend wise investment choices.

Trust. Trust will never go out of style. It's a fundamental component of building a close, long-term personal relationship with your clients.

Your clients must always feel that you do what's in their best interest and that they can trust you completely. Don't merely behave with integrity, but communicate with them so well that you're the first professional they think of when it comes to making financial choices. Show them how much you appreciate their business, get interested in their life, and always be up front with them. That's going to give you clients for life.

Take some time to reflect how much real, sustainable value you provide to your clients. Are you giving them the kind of service that they just can't get elsewhere? Is the value you provide worth what you're charging, or can people find it elsewhere for a lower price? If you're not working on creating more time in your clients' life, being their primary source of financial wisdom, and building trust with them, you can't build an unassailable brand.

I Stands for Intimacy

Great brands create intimacy. One of the keys to being successful in this business (and life in general) is to develop intimate relationships that last. And it's not just your relationship with your clients but your staff's relationship with them as well. In fact, your staff may come in contact more often with your clients than you will, so they have to be part of the intimacy-building process too.

Brands are built not just on what you say but on what you do. Each and every point of contact with your clients and prospects sends a message. It can either add or detract from the relationship you're building. Keep that in mind as you think about your office space, how you answer the phone, how you greet your clients, the way you dress, and how you conduct your meetings.

Here are eight ways you can deepen your client relationships and show them genuine appreciation, care, support, respect, and a desire to help and serve:

1. **Birthday call.** You will be amazed at the power of calling your clients on their birthday. It is a very simple act, yet it is genuinely appreciated by the receiver and will separate you from most other advisors.

2. **Greeting card.** When you send your client a holiday card or greeting card, make it a special one. By this we mean not to send a card that comes from a box of cards that all look the same. Send a personalized card that will have meaning to the person you are sending it to. Add a personalized note to make it really special.

3. **Spouse birthday flowers.** For your female clients and for your male clients' spouse, send them flowers on their birthday. Flowers brighten their day as well as their opinion of you and your firm.

4. **Wedding anniversary.** For your male clients, call them one week ahead of their wedding anniversary and remind them

that it's coming up. Unfortunately, some men tend to let this date slip so that by reminding them, you may save them from the dog house.

5. **Random acts of kindness.** For no reason other than your genuine appreciation of your clients, do something special for them. Be sincere and you'll put a smile on their faces that will light up their life.

6. **Retirement party.** If you have a client who is retiring, throw him or her a surprise retirement party. Imagine the look on the client's face when he or she sees you are the one behind it!

7. **Special luncheon.** Invite your A+ clients to a special luncheon. And when you do, ask each of them to invite a friend.

8. **Handwritten notes.** In the age of e-mail, the lost art of the handwritten note is more appreciated than ever. Get in the habit of sending your clients handwritten notes and thank-you letters, and they will be the ones thanking you.

Of course, you can think of other ideas too, but this list should give you a good start. As you do these things, keep in mind *why* you are doing them. Your motivation should be pure, genuine, and sincere; if it's not, then don't do them. Although client loyalty and referrals are not your objectives (remember this is done out of kindness and love), they will be the result.

You may say that these "special things" have nothing to do with putting together quality plans for clients that meet their goals and objectives. That's true, but your job is more than just numbers. We assume you are already delivering high-quality planning advice. Think of this intimacy as an added dimension you bring to your client relationships that distinguishes you from all other advisors. These special gestures will cement your client relationships and remind your clients that you don't view them as simply the source of your income but rather as people whom you can serve and delight.

Ultimately, every aspect of your business should work in concert to add intimacy to the relationship you have with your clients.

P Stands for Personality

Great brands are infused with the company's personality. In this case, you are the company, so it needs to be infused with your unique personality. For example, you may be a health and fitness enthusiast. If so, you may want to do client events that revolve around health and fitness; you may want to include a few health and fitness tips on your Web site. Your brochure may include pictures of healthy-looking people engaged in sporting activities.

Or perhaps you're a strong believer in educating your clients about the vagaries of the market so they don't panic when things get rough. In this case, you might publish a short weekly educational newsletter for your clients. You also may want to have a wide variety of educational pieces on your Web site. And for each of your new clients, you may have them go through a two- or three-step educational program that equips them with basic financial information so they can feel more confident in their financial decision making.

If you're not sure what your company's personality is, try this. Make sure you and your staff answer this question: If your business were a TV show, which one would it be? For example, would it be *Survivor* because you're just fighting to stay alive in the business? Would it be *Who Wants to Be a Millionaire* because you're constantly chasing the money? Or would it be *The Apprentice* because your clients keep telling you "You're fired"? If you and your staff come up with different shows, then you've got a problem. You probably have blurred vision, making it hard for people to connect with you and your vision.

Take a cue from Hollywood. The biggest stars have a personality that attracts attention. Take your positive personality attributes, infuse them into your practice, and you'll help define your brand.

E Stands for Experience

Great brands make you feel pampered and special. Twenty years ago, coffee was a cheap, bland product that people didn't think twice about. They just drank it as part of their daily routine for the caffeine jolt. Today, drinking coffee is a communal, sense-pleasing experience that enriches people's life. Of course, we have Starbucks to thank for that.

When you walk into a Starbucks, you can smell the aroma of the rich beans, hear the whir of the stainless steel coffee machines, lose yourself in the art on the wall, and take refuge from the stress of work. It's a unique experience that comforts and soothes, a gathering place for family and friends. It's a way to bond for only $4.

You could save a lot of money and pay $1 for a cup of coffee at a fast-food place but it's not the same. Starbucks is a great example of the truism that people will gladly pay a significant premium for an experience. What are you doing to create an experience in your business?

R Stands for Respect

Great brands command respect in the marketplace. They've built this respect by having a history of meeting or exceeding expectations, by staying true to core values, and by doing things the right way. Obviously, being respected is a critical ingredient to being a successful financial advisor. By always taking the high road and doing what's in the best interest of your clients, you'll lay the foundation for being a respected advisor and add to the value of your brand.

The Grateful Dead and VIPER

One of the most enduring music groups of all-time is a great example of the VIPER strategy in action. The Grateful Dead lasted 30 years from the turbulent 1960s through the mid-1990s and along the way developed a legion of fanatical followers who loved the band through thick and thin. Even though The Grateful Dead have nothing to do with financial services, they broke the traditional rules of the music business and became a huge success. We want to share how they did it within the context of the VIPER strategy as a way of showing you that the traditional way of building a business—whether it's in music or financial services—is not the only way.

Vision. Former President George Bush may not have gotten the "vision thing," but The Grateful Dead did. They had a clear vision for their music, which was developed during the counterculture, drug-crazed 1960s and continued until lead guitarist Jerry Garcia's death in 1995. The band's musical vision combined blues, rock, country, and folk with a splash of psychedelic. It was a compelling vision that attracted the young, the old, the rich, and the poor.

Values. One of The Grateful Dead's core values was to stay true to their music. Despite the public's shifting musical tastes from antiwar anthems to disco to punk to rap, the band never changed. They knew who they were, and they stayed focused on the integrity of their music concert after concert. They never compromised.

Value. Grateful Dead concerts would sometimes last for hours as Garcia and his mates jammed the night away. Nobody walked away feeling they didn't get their money's worth.

Intimacy. The band created an intimate community with their fans. In fact, the fans felt so close to the band and were so proud to be part of the culture that they called themselves Dead Heads. Many of the Dead Heads attended dozens of shows. Why? Because each one was different. The band would play different songs; Jerry Garcia would mess up the lyrics or stop in the middle of a song if he didn't like how it was going. You'd never know what would happen at the concert so an aura built up around them. Concertgoers would share stories about what had happened at earlier concerts. They'd try to guess what songs would be played and so on. The band even let concertgoers tape their shows. This fan-friendly action allowed the fans to get even closer to the band.

Personality. From their six-hour concerts to their innovative and colorful album covers to their enigmatic stage presence, The Grateful Dead infused their brand with a unique personality that helped define an era. When you think of the 1960s, things like drugs, psychedelic music, and Haight-Ashbury come to mind. And nobody epitomizes that more than the Dead. Their personality was so strong that it still resonates 40 years later.

Experience. The Grateful Dead created a unique experience that was like no other. Their rambling concerts, light shows, and eclectic music kept their fans turned on and tuned in for years. In fact, the late rock music promoter Bill Graham commented about the band: "They're not the best at what they do; they're the only ones who do what they do." The band thrived on live concerts, and it was during the shows that they bonded with their fans and created an unforgettable experience.

Respect. Whether or not you liked the band's music, you had to respect them for their fan dedication and their single-minded focus on their musical style. They knew who they were, and they kept delivering it year after year.

Like the pieces of a puzzle, the band's success was a combination of dozens of actions all joined together that created the relationship between the band and its fans. This relationship was so strong that despite only one top-ten song in 30 years, The Grateful Dead generated millions of fans who were in love with the band and in love with the feeling they got by being part of the culture.

Your job as a financial advisor is actually much easier than The Grateful Dead's job because you're not looking for millions of fans. You're only looking for about 150. If The Grateful Dead can create lasting value to millions of fans over a 30-year period, just imagine what you can do for 150 clients.

Get Noticed

You could be the world's best financial advisor, the most technically sound, and the most trusted, but if nobody knows about you, you're history. The other component of branding is to get the word out. Share your story with your target audience. Let it know who you are, what you do, how you do it, and why you're different. The two key ways to do that are through the spoken word and the printed word.

When it comes to public speaking, you have two options. First, you can create your own audience by setting up financial workshops and marketing them through direct mail, e-mail, and co-sponsors. These can work as long as you have a compelling topic, good delivery style, and an organized system that results in appointments. The second option is to find local organizations that already have an audience of people you'd like to have as clients. When you find these organizations, call their meeting organizer and ask if you can speak on a topic that is relevant and adds value. This route entails less cost and organization on your part yet can still be effective.

The printed word is also one of the most effective ways to get your firm noticed. Start writing articles for your local newspaper or for some industry- or trade-specific periodicals that cater to the types of clients you are looking for. Publishing articles can help you become known as an expert. It may not result in immediate business, but when the time is right, your name will be top of mind, and you'll likely get the first call.

Any type of communication you do helps get you noticed and adds to your brand. But remember, all communication is a point of contact, so make sure it's professional, coordinated, and consistent with the message you're trying to send.

Position Yourself as a Wealth Advisor

As part of your brand, you want to be perceived as the "go-to" person for wealthy people. You need to position your firm as the solution for wealthy peoples' financial needs. To get there, you have to understand that there's a certain pecking order in the financial services industry. If you want to work with wealthy clients, you have to offer similar services—but at a higher level and with a deeper relationship—compared with the other advisors working in your segment.

Although there are numerous ways to segment wealthy people, here's one of the most common:

Ultrahigh Net Worth	$30+ million Investable Assets
Decamillionaires	$10+ million Investable Assets
Pentamillionaires	$5+ million Investable Assets
Affluent	$500,000+ Investable Assets
The Vast Mass	$50,000+ Investable Assets

Notice the chart is based on *investable* assets. The net worth of many of these people is probably substantially higher because of their having assets tied up in a business or real estate. So let's see who you have a reasonable shot at working with and how you can position yourself to be attractive to them.

The Ultrahigh Net Worth mostly work with old-line trust companies or family offices. They have an overall net worth that could easily reach $100 million or even the billions. Realistically, your chances of working with them are slim.

Next in line are the Decamillionaires. With $10 million or more in investable assets, these people probably have a net worth that ranges up to $100 million. Most of them are probably served by trust companies, full-time personal advisors, and, to some extent, major wire houses. You may occasionally come across a prospect like this, but it definitely won't become your bread and butter.

Most million-dollar producers have some Pentamillionaires in their book. You may not have all their investable assets because they frequently have multiple advisors. For most advisors, building your business around Pentamillionaires is not a good idea, because Pentamillionaires are few and far between, and there's no single strategy to effectively attract them.

The Affluent are the bread and butter for the typical successful advisor. They're the "millionaire next door" and are easily within reach of every competent, professional advisor.

The Vast Mass are best left to advisors who are new to the business and to Associate Advisors on your staff.

So the sweetspot is the Affluent category, those with $500,000 or more in investable assets. In addition to doing everything else recommended in this book, you become attractive to affluent people by positioning yourself as a Wealth Advisor.

A Wealth Advisor is a competent, caring professional capable of "quarterbacking" a client's entire financial situation. This means that through your firm you can offer retirement planning, investments, and insurance, tax, and estate planning. It doesn't mean you personally have to offer all these services. But it does mean you have these experts on staff or you have preestablished relationships with outside professionals who can work closely with your clients under your direction and control.

If you don't have these experts on staff, set up an alliance relationship with them, but make sure they come to your office for client meetings. You lose a tremendous amount of value when your clients have to go to the attorney's office or the CPA's office. The value is generated by having clients go to one place (your office) for all their meetings and having one professional coordinating all their financial needs.

Clients need to know they can come to your firm and get all of their financial needs taken care of in a seamless, proactive manner, but that doesn't mean all your clients will take advantage of it. Some clients come to you with preexisting professional relationships that they don't want to sever. That's fine. In those situations, let the clients know that your firm can work with their other advisors to make sure clients' entire financial position is well coordinated.

Once you have your wealth team assembled, you have to communicate it. There are at least five ways to get the word out:

1. Send a letter and e-mail to all your clients announcing the new services.
2. Let your clients know what's available as you meet with them for reviews.
3. Mention the new services when you make your monthly and quarterly touch-base calls.
4. Send a press release to the local media.
5. Have a client event with your other professionals as guest speakers.

By offering all the financial services generally needed by wealthy people and effectively communicating it, you can position yourself to become attractive to the demographic you are targeting.

The Power of First Impressions

One of the key factors in successfully selling a home is to make sure the home has "curb appeal." Curb appeal is the view that prospective buyers see when they drive by the home. If their first impression isn't favorable, the brake pedal is never touched, and you've missed a potential sale.

It's no different in our business.

People are so starved for time today that they use the first impression as a time management tool. If they don't immediately like what they see or hear, they're gone. Roger Ailes, a business executive and media consultant to the late President Ronald Reagan, says we have only seven seconds to make a good first impression. Based on our experience, in the first three seconds you can form an impression about how someone looks, how somehow is groomed, and how someone smiles (or doesn't smile). In the next four seconds, you can hear the individual speak, feel how the person shakes hands, and gauge his or her level of confidence and sophistication. That's all it takes, seven seconds to make or break a relationship.

So what are you doing with your seven seconds?

There are two areas we'd like to discuss. First, how can you improve your personal first impression, and, second, how can you improve the first impression of all the points of contact in your organization?

Improving the Impression of *You*

When prospects meet you in person, that first impression of you is just like the one of the house hunter—it's your curb appeal. They then interpret this curb appeal reaction through their own lens. It's not based on a rational, in-depth analysis but rather based simply on the instincts and emotions that have been developed over years of experience. What they see in you is matched up with their own biases of what people with your curb appeal are really like. If you make a positive first impression—great—you've passed the first hurdle. If you make a poor one—shame on you—it will take a long time to change it.

Here are five steps you can take to make that first impression of you a positive one:

1. **Dress for success.** Let's face it, how you dress speaks volumes about you. If you pay little attention to your clothing, people assume you pay little attention to everything else. Few of us are born with a fashion sense, so consider working with a wardrobe consultant. A consultant can help you purchase clothes and accessories that match your body type and skin color and are fashionable and professional. And be sure to shine your shoes!

2. **Show your pearly whites.** A genuine, heartfelt smile makes people warm up to you and triggers a positive impression. In fact, in Dale Carnegie's book *How to Win Friends and Influence People,* he cites smiling as one of the six ways to make people like you. A smile to a stranger is the emotional equivalent of embracing an old friend, so don't be stingy flexing your face muscles.

3. **Project confidence.** Your posture plays a big role in how people perceive your level of confidence. When you stand, stand tall. Keep a straight line from your ears down to your ankles. Relax your shoulders and bend your knees slightly so you don't look too stiff. When you sit, don't slouch. Keep your hips as far back in the chair as possible. As a side benefit, good posture puts less strain on your body and allows you to work more efficiently with less fatigue.

4. **Meet eye-to-eye.** There's nothing worse than people who won't look you in the eye. Even if they won't look in your eyes, look in theirs. Of course, don't stare or you may come

across as intimidating. Meeting them eye-to-eye says, "I'm interested in what you are saying, I'm communicating directly with you, and you are important to me." What a great way to start a relationship.

5. **Speak authoritatively.** Your voice is a powerful communication tool that adds to or detracts from your presence. You could be dressed to kill, but if your voice doesn't match the way you look, you're sunk. Through training, you can develop a great speaking voice. Work with a professional and practice the fundamentals of breathing, resonance, articulation, pitch, and body language.

Improving the Impression of All Your Points of Contact

Make every point of contact with your firm an opportunity to delight your clients and prospects and reinforce why they are, or should be, doing business with you.

Here's an exercise we'd like you to do. Pretend for a moment that you are a prospect and then drive into the parking lot of your office. Grab a pad of paper and a pen and start walking toward your office door. Be observant and make notes about any positive or negative impressions you have as you approach your office. Is the landscaping professional? Is the paint fresh? Is there garbage on the ground? Are cigarette butts lying around? Is the door easy or hard to open?

Make your way inside the building and then stop in your office's reception area. Take a close look around. Look at the floor, the walls, the furniture, the lighting, the cleanliness, the "feel" of the area. Are you pleasantly surprised at how nice everything looks or are you uncomfortably disappointed? Take good notes.

Next, walk through your entire office and visually inspect everything. Remember, you're a prospect now, and you're trying to determine if this office is generating a positive first impression for you. Take good notes.

Ask your staff to do this same exercise. When everybody has finished this "visual audit," get your team together and compare notes. At this team meeting, review all the other points of contact in your practice too. For example, review how you answer the phone, the quality of your brochure and stationery, and the professionalism of your Web site. Figure out ways to dramatically elevate the visual impression people experience when they first come in contact with you and your firm.

One area that deserves extra attention is the office dress code. Until the mid-1990s, business dress tended to be suits and ties for men and comparable attire for women. Then the tech boom began, and the casualness of Silicon Valley caught hold, and many firms switched to a casual dress code for business. Today, the trend has reversed.

Dr. Jeffrey L. Magee, a research psychologist, surveyed 500 firms between 1997 and 1998 and found that companies that adopted a casual dress code experienced the following:

- An increase in tardiness, absenteeism, and early departures
- An increase in foul language and inappropriate conversation
- An increase in provocative actions, which led to more complaints to HR and consequently to more litigation
- A decrease in polite, mannerly behavior
- A decrease in productivity and overall quality of work
- A decrease in commitment and company loyalty

In our experience, casual dress generates casual results. Our firm recently switched back to a formal dress code. Men now wear suits and ties, and women wear comparable clothes. Professional dress is one point of contact over which you have total control, so don't waste it by dressing down.

Ron recently visited the home office of his broker-dealer and noticed that everybody—including the mailroom staff—wore professional business attire. This policy was set by the company's founder, who said, "If you want to dress casual, go work at Gap." *Touché!*

SUMMARY

- Branding is demanding. An effective brand is demanded by its consumers.
- By consciously incorporating your uniqueness into the VIPER™ brand strategy, executing a strategy to get noticed, and positioning yourself as a Wealth Advisor, you can create an in-demand brand that attracts the right kind of people to you.
- You could be the world's best financial advisor, the most technically sound, and the most trusted—but if nobody knows about you, you're history. The other component of branding is to get the word out. Share your story with your target audience. Let it know who you are, what you do, how you do it, and why you're different. The two key ways to do that are through the spoken word and the printed word.
- People are so starved for time today that they use their first impression as a time management tool. If they don't immediately like what they see or hear, they're gone. Make every point of contact with your firm an opportunity to delight your clients and prospects and reinforce why they are, or should be, doing business with you.
- In our experience, casual dress generates casual results. Our firm recently switched back to a formal dress code. If you want to wear casual attire, work at Gap.

TNT #5 ACTION STEPS

- Figure out what your current brand is by asking five of your clients this question: "Mr. and Mrs. _____, when you hear the name of my firm, what do you think of?" If the response is not what you want to hear, then work on implementing the VIPER branding strategy.

- Make a strong effort to get noticed by speaking in public and getting published.

- Position yourself as a Wealth Advisor by bringing in-house, or affiliating yourself with, professionals in the tax and estate planning areas. Make sure your office can act as a quarterback for your clients' entire financial situation.

- Improve your first impression by:
  - Improving your dress
  - Smiling more often
  - Projecting confidence
  - Making good eye contact
  - Speaking authoritatively

- Perform a "visual audit" of your office, and make the appropriate improvements to enhance the first impression others receive of your office environment.

- Review and improve every point of contact (stationery, letters, marketing material, etc.) with your clients and prospects.

BUILD RELATIONSHIPS AND COMMUNICATE

12

REACH OUT AND TOUCH
YOUR CLIENTS AND PROSPECTS

"Those who bring sunshine to the lives of others cannot keep it from themselves."
—JAMES BARRIE

What's the difference between an account and a relationship? According to Ron:

> An account is reactive. It's when your client calls you to discuss something you should already know about. A relationship is proactive. You call your client about something before they've had the opportunity to ask you about it or even before they knew they had the need. You're anticipating their needs, staying on top of the situation, and exceeding their expectations.

> Go through your list of clients and ask yourself, Do they have an account with me, or do they have a relationship with me? You won't double or triple your business by getting more accounts; you'll double or triple your business by getting more relationships. But not just any relationships. That's where profiling your clients comes in.

PROFILING YOUR CLIENTS

As mentioned earlier, physically, mentally, and emotionally we're capable of developing solid relationships with about 150 people. With that in mind, you have to be choosy when it comes to whom you do business with. The first place to start is your own client base. You have to profile and segment your clients into categories that reflect their impact on your business and your desire to work with them. This is accomplished through a process we call *profiling your clients.*

The first step is to understand that there are five types of clients:

1. A+ Clients

These are your very best clients. You may currently have only one or two. These clients are A+ because they have a lot of money invested with you and because of the quality of referrals they can provide. They come from all walks of life. They also have many gatekeepers, which is good because once you're in, it makes it hard for somebody else to get in and push you out. You get 100 A, B, C, or D clients through marketing before you get an A+. The key to getting A+ clients is through referrals.

2. A Clients

These clients are successful professionals, affluent retirees, and small business owners. Their net worth is generally in the seven figures, and their incomes are generally in the six figures. These are people you also want to clone, and they will make up the backbone of your business.

3. B Clients

B clients are similar to A clients, but they don't have as much money invested with you. The objective here is to promote these B clients to A clients by spending more time profiling and gathering assets that you don't have. We found that one reason you may not have all their business is that you simply haven't established full credibility with them, or they don't perceive you as someone who can handle their entire financial situation. Just because someone is a B client this year doesn't mean he or she is going to be a B client forever. Your job is to uncover all the assets. This takes time and comes from establishing long-term relationships that are built on the highest levels of trust, integrity, and service. Longer term, your B clients should be handed off to an Associate Wealth Advisor in your office.

4. C Clients

Your C clients are those who generate very little income for you. And not only that, they probably consume a disproportional amount of your time and headaches. Your best strategy is to have them work with an Associate Wealth Advisor in your office. Notice we didn't suggest you "fire" them. Just because they have little money with you is not a good reason to fire them. We believe if you brought them on as a client, you have an ethical obligation to keep them because they were there when you needed them. However, by having them work with one of your associates, you can structure it so they consume very little of your time.

5. D Clients

These clients are not D clients because of their account size. They're D clients because you don't like them and they don't like you. You know who we're talking about. As Ron likes to say: "When you get a message that they called, you get a sick, sinking feeling in your stomach, and you wait until the last possible minute to return the call." They may even have a significant amount of money with you, but that's not the point. The point is, no matter what you do, you can't satisfy them. Your performance is never good enough. Your service is never timely. You're never available when they want you. As a result, you're miserable dealing with them— and they're unhappy too.

This type of client does need to be fired regardless of his or her account size. It's not an ethical issue. It's just a situation where you have a really bad fit, and you and the client would be much better off parting ways.

Here's an example from Ron:

A few years ago, I had a client open a $4 million asset management account with me. I knew from the start that he probably wasn't the best fit for me, but I figured I could find a way to make it work. Shortly after he came on board, my staff came to me to advise we needed to fire him because he was abusive, unreasonable, and uncooperative. So I called him and explained the problems that my staff were having with him. He quickly assured me that he would change his ways, so I let him stay.

A little later, my staff came back to me to report he was still a problem, and that if I were really serious when I said I'd fire clients that were problems, then this guy had to go. With no choice left, I called him again and said that my company is not able to meet his expectations, and therefore I would like him to transfer his account. He was incredulous and said, "You mean to tell me you're asking me to move my $4 million account to another advisor?" I said, "Yes, and I can hardly believe it myself."

So he left, the staff felt better, and I learned the importance of working only with people who are a good fit for you and your staff.

As you look at each client level, where you draw the line determines how high your income will go. For example, your categorization may look like this:

- A+ client: $1 million or more invested with you or a major center of influence or at least a $5 million net worth
- A client: $500,000 to $1 million invested with you
- B client: $100,000 to $500,000 invested with you
- C client: Less than $100,000 invested with you

You can adjust these levels to suit your practice. However, keep in mind that accounts of less than $100,000 are not going to be profitable, so don't accept accounts below that.

The second step in profiling your clients—the first step is understanding there are five types or categories of clients as described above—is to segment your clients into the five categories. To do that, go through your entire client list and (1) list all your clients by portfolio size, (2) make your first ranking according to portfolio size, (3) review the list and promote clients who could potentially move up to a new level, and (4) promote clients who are large centers of influence.

The third step is to create a description of your ideal client. What is the ideal age, income, net worth, risk level, occupation, hobbies, and interests? Write down a one-paragraph description of your ideal client and read it from time to time to remind yourself of the type of client you are looking for.

The final step is to determine your goal for the average account size per relationship. Consider the quality of life you want, how many hours you want to work, how many clients you can service, your income goal, and your average revenue per million of assets. With this information, you can solve the average account size using this formula:

$$(I \div C) \div R \times 1{,}000{,}000$$

where I = income goal, C = target number of clients, and R = revenue per million in assets.

The resulting number should be your target average account size per relationship. For example, let's say your income goal is $750,000, your target number of clients is 150, and your revenue per million in assets is $10,000. Using the formula, your target average account size is $500,000.

Once you've segmented your clients, you can focus on building relationships with your A+ and A clients, because those are the people who will help you get to the next level.

IT'S ALL ABOUT RELATIONSHIPS

Our industry has evolved dramatically over the years. Back in the 1970s and early '80s, it was all about hard assets. Tax shelters were very popular and most brokers were simply in the transaction business. Clients were viewed as accounts. In the late 1980s to the mid-1990s, packaged products and managed accounts became all the rage. Sales and distribution became king as Schwab, Fidelity, and their ilk became big aggregators of assets. In the late 1990s, the Internet took over and commoditized any informational advantage financial advisors had.

Today, financial advisors must turn to the only thing left that cannot be commoditized, cannot be mass produced, and cannot be cheapened by the Internet. It's called a *relationship*. There's no technology, no marketing gimmick, and no invention that's going to make relationships obsolete—and that's your advantage.

If you lined up all your clients in a row, would you be able to greet each of them by their first name? Would you feel comfortable hugging them? Many financial advisors have too many accounts and not enough relationships. So how many relationships can you comfortably have? As we mentioned earlier, somewhere in the neighborhood of 150 is about right. If you get too far above 150, you start to lose the personal connection. Think about that number the next time you are tempted to add a client. Do you want that client for life? Do you want to develop a connection with that client that transcends a business-to-consumer relationship? If not, save the spot for someone else.

How do you develop relationships?

For starters, developing relationships with clients is not a strategy, a tactic, or a gimmick. It's simply being human. In this post–9/11 era, people crave connection. People want genuine relationships with other human beings, and as a financial advisor, you are in a unique position to develop client relationships. Why? Because you are entrusted with one of your clients' innermost secrets—their money.

Have you ever noticed how people go on TV and talk about everything imaginable in their personal life except their money? Money is really the last taboo. But as a financial advisor, you're trusted with the money. As a result, you have the ability to get really close to your clients; uncover their hopes, dreams, and aspirations in life; and then, through thoughtful financial planning, help deliver a solution that takes them from where they are today to where they want to be tomorrow.

It's an enviable position that comes with great responsibility.

ASK GREAT QUESTIONS

Developing a trusting, connective relationship with your clients first and foremost involves being genuine and sincere. You have to have a sincere interest in wanting to know more about your clients. When you look at them, you have to see a human being, not a dollar sign. With that established, the relationship begins by asking good questions.

Let's pretend for a moment that the tables are turned. Instead of being the advisor, you're now the client. In the capacity of being a client, ask yourself, What do I want my financial advisor to know about me that will help him or her build a better financial plan? Think about your answer for a moment. Now put your financial advisor hat back on. Are you asking your clients the questions that would elicit the information you wanted *your* financial advisor to know about you? If not, why not?

There are two types of information you can gather about your clients—quantitative and qualitative. Most advisors are well versed in gathering the quantitative information. Where the breakdown occurs is in gathering the qualitative information. Think of it this way. The quantitative information is like skin color; there are a few basic colors, and everything else is just a slight variation of a basic color. Figuring out your clients' skin color (i.e., risk tolerance, goals, assets, liabilities, etc.) is the easy part. Qualitative information, on the other hand, is more like DNA; there are billions and billions of combinations, and that is what makes each of us unique. Your role is to decode your clients' DNA and understand exactly what makes them who they are. When you understand their DNA, you can develop custom solutions that match their individual needs.

Just as DNA is composed of five basic elements (carbon, hydrogen, nitrogen, oxygen, and phosphorus for the scientifically interested), your questions should revolve around five areas: Background, Values, Vision, Legacy, and Objectives. Following are questions you should ask in each of these areas to unlock your clients' DNA:

Background (Understand your clients' past and what caused them to be sitting in front of you at this moment.)

1. **Tell me a little bit about your background. Where are you from? How did you get into your present career?** Based on their response to these questions, you should have a series of follow-up questions that prompt them to open up even more and share their past with you. Ideally, try to find some common background. For example, did you go to the same high school or college? Do you live in the same neighborhood? Do you have some acquaintances in common?

2. **As you look back on your life, what role has money played in it? Have you worked with a financial advisor in the past, and, if so, what kind of experience did you have?** Through these questions and appropriate follow-up questions, you should try to uncover any concerns, issues, or successes they've had with money and how that shapes their life. You'll want to find out if they had any negative experiences with money. For example, maybe they grew up very poor, and their biggest fear now is losing what money they have.

3. **What are some of the important things that have happened in your life that will help me put together a better plan for you?** This is a catch-all question that should bring out any issues you need to be aware of. You can also use this question as an opportunity to explore other transitions clients may have been through or are going through in their life.

Values (Understand what's important to your clients and how that may impact your financial plan for them.)

1. **What are a few of the things you value most in life?** Values are the things we cherish most; they characterize who we are and how we conduct ourselves. Your goal is to try and understand your clients' values system so you can incorporate/accommodate them in your planning process. For example, health may be a cherished value, and, as a result, you may not want to invest in Krispy Kreme Doughnuts stock.

2. **What event or occurrence in your life significantly moved you?** Their response to this question offers insight into what shaped them as a person.
3. **What did you/do you teach your children about the value of money?** Knowing what your clients teach their children about money helps you understand how your clients feel about money.

Vision (Understand your client's hopes, dreams, and aspirations for their future lifestyle.)

1. **If money were not an issue, what would your ideal lifestyle be? Where would you live? With whom would you surround yourself?** One of your jobs is to try and help your clients move closer to their ideal lifestyle by providing them with expert advice, guidance, and thoughtful financial planning.
2. **If you had all the money you ever needed, what would give you purpose and motivate you throughout the day?** This gets to the core of their purpose in life. Once you know that, you can help them arrange their finances so they can spend more of their time in the area that brings them purpose.
3. **How do you define success?** Knowing the answer to this question helps you develop a customized plan that is targeted to meet your clients' definition of success.

Legacy (Understand the mark your clients would like to leave in this world.)

1. **What would you like to accomplish while you still can?** Here you'll learn if there are any loose ends in their life that they need to tie up. For example, perhaps they want to take that once-in-a-lifetime trip. If you know that, you can help prepare them financially to make it a reality.

2. **What impact would you like your estate to have after you're gone?** For clients with significant wealth, here's an opportunity for them to share with you what they hope their money can accomplish after they're gone. Armed with this knowledge, you can develop a plan to help them accomplish it.

3. **If you could pass on one secret of life for all future generations, what would that secret be?** Here you'll learn what wisdom they value, and you'll understand more about what makes them tick.

Objectives (Understand specifically what your clients hope to achieve.)

1. **What's the number one issue you'd like help with right now?** With this question, you establish that they have a need. From there, your job is to learn more about the issue and help them with it.

2. **Are you more concerned about growing your assets or protecting what you already have?** With this simple risk question, you can cut through a lot of clutter.

3. **What has to happen over the next few years for you to feel our relationship has been successful?** By answering this, your clients give you a road map to a successful relationship.

These 15 questions, when asked with sincerity and genuineness, will enrich your client relationships. As we said in our introduction, our business is not about products. It's about people. Focus on the people first, connect with them, understand their needs at a core level, and then develop and deliver solutions that fit and work.

THE POWER OF STORYTELLING

Have you ever met with prospects who nodded their heads in agreement throughout your conversation, but then said they had to "think about it" before doing business with you? If so, you've been a victim of "half-brain connectedness." You connected only with the left half of their brains—the linear and logical side, the side that needs facts and figures. No doubt you wowed prospects with alphas and betas and historical rates of return, but, unfortunately, that's only half of the story.

The right half of the brain is the emotional and creative side, the side that helps you form a bond with prospects. To really connect with prospects, you have to meet the needs of both sides of the brain. Stories are your path to "whole-brain connectedness."

Stories simplify complex ideas. Stories are received and processed. Stories are multidimensional. Stories last long after they are told. Stories reach the heart in a way facts and figures cannot.

Prospects don't want to be sold. They want to buy. Stories don't sell. Instead, they allow people to make their own interpretation, apply it to their life, and then make an informed decision about doing business with you. Stories unify the two halves of the brain so prospects can feel they have enough facts to satisfy their logical needs and enough feelings to satisfy their emotional needs. The end result is happily engaged new clients.

As you develop your stories, consider incorporating some or all of the following pieces:

- Set the stage for the story.
- Vividly describe who's involved in the story.
- Describe the obstacle or conflict in the story.
- Overcome the obstacle or conflict.
- Make your point.

Storytelling is an art that can take years to refine. But most important, it requires genuineness and authenticity. It's not a tool for manipulation. It's a tool for communication and relationship building. Be clear about who you are and what you stand for and then passionately communicate that in the stories you tell.

If you want to learn more about how to become a better storyteller, Steve highly recommends the book *The Story Factor* (Perseus Books, 2002) by Annette Simmons.

COMMUNICATION

Like a great marriage, a successful advisor-client relationship requires frequent and clear communication.

Industry studies suggest you should communicate with your clients somewhere between 18 to 30 times a year. At Carson Wealth Management Group, Ron communicates with his A+ clients more than 75 times a year. He never wants to lose a client from neglect, so he's developed systems to make sure that doesn't happen.

The goal is to stay "top of mind" with your clients. When your clients have a financial need, your name should be the only one that comes to mind. To make that happen, you need to communicate, communicate, communicate. In addition to staying top of mind, proactive client communication builds loyalty and helps you detect potential problems long before they become unfixable.

The key to staying top of mind is to vary your method of communication. No client wants you to call him or her 75 times a year, so mix it up. Following are seven key ways you can communicate with your clients.

1. Weekly Commentary

The weekly commentary is the cornerstone of the Carson Wealth communication program. Every Monday, clients and prospects receive via e-mail a weekly commentary that reviews the previous week's market activity and adds a colorful, nonmarket-related story. The commentary also contains the Carson Wealth team picture and company contact information. There are three objectives to be achieved with the commentary. First, because it is sent 52 times per year, it keeps the firm top of mind. Second, it lets our clients know we're staying on top of the market situation, and it enhances our credibility. And third, by adding a nonmarket-related story, it humanizes the commentary and lets our personality shine through.

We write the commentary in-house each weekend, have it approved through our Compliance department Monday morning, and then e-mail it Monday afternoon. It's relevant, timely, and has been a huge home run for us. It works because it's personal. A broker-dealer's commentary or another institutionally written commentary will not have nearly the same effect because they're too sterile. Figure 12.1 shows an example of our commentary.

Because the commentary is sent via e-mail, the delivery cost is very low. And the low delivery cost makes the commentary an attractive way to stay top of mind, not just with clients, but with prospects and the media as well. We aggressively add prospects and media contacts to our e-mail list, the perfect way to stay in touch with a prospect who may not have a need for your services now but could in the future. A fine example would be people you meet in a social setting. You wouldn't ask everyone you meet at a dinner party to set up an appointment with you, but you could very easily mention the market commentary, get the e-mail addresses of several guests, and add them to the list. Instead of looking like a needy salesperson, you're now viewed as an expert market commentator sharing information.

This works great with the media too. By adding media contacts to your list, you add to your credibility, stay top of mind, and will likely be the first person these contacts call when they have a question about market volatility, new tax changes, and the like. Pretty soon you'll start getting quoted in the media and begin increasing your name recognition within your community.

FIGURE 12.1 *Sample Commentary*

[Insert team picture and contact information.]

Weekly Commentary
August 2, 2004

The Markets

Is the market missing something or is it telling us something?

The answer to that question depends on whether you're bullish or bearish. The bulls would say the market's malaise over the past seven months is unjustified because of the solid growth in corporate earnings and the turnaround in the job market. But the bears would counter by saying the malaise correctly anticipated a new rising interest rate cycle, slowing (but still solid) earnings growth, and the ever-present danger of terrorism and its associated effects such as higher oil prices.

So who's right?

In reality, the question of who's right is really not an important question to answer. What's important is that we have both bulls and bears. At its most elemental level, it's bulls and bears that make markets. Someone bullish buys a share from someone who is bearish and we have a trade. That happens thousands of times a day. Sometimes, the bulls are a little more aggressive and the price gets bid up. Other times, the bears are in charge and the price goes down. Where we run into trouble is when the herd instinct takes over and we have too many bulls or too many bears.

When the bull herd is in charge, we may end up with a technology bubble like the one we witnessed in the late 1990s. The denouement of that was devastating for many people. When the bear herd is in charge, we may end up with a crash like the one we witnessed in October 1987. Either way, a herding market is not good.

That's why the current standoff between bulls and bears, although frustrating in the short term, is actually healthy. It suggests investors are carefully weighing the pros and cons and concluding that the market may be reasonably priced. Our hope is that as the election year draws to a close, the bulls will eventually gain a slight majority and gradually move the market higher. In the meantime, we will continue to look for opportunities for upside growth and to diversify for downside protection.

Returns through 7/30/04	1-Week	Y-T-D	1-Year	3-Year	5-Year	10-Year
Dow Jones Industrials	1.8%	−3.0%	10.8	−1.2%	−1.0%	10.3%
Nasdaq Composite	2.1	−5.8	10.0	−2.4	−6.4	10.0
Standard & Poor's 500	1.4	−0.9	12.4	−3.1	−3.7	9.1
Dow Jones World (Ex. U.S.)	0.6	0.5	23.9	3.3	−1.9	N/A

Source: Yahoo! Finance, Barrons

Past performance is no guarantee of future results. Indices are unmanaged and cannot be invested into directly; 3-, 5-, and 10-year returns are annualized.

(continued)

FIGURE 12.1 *Sample Commentary, continued*

Did we really have a recession in 2001? According to the official arbiter of such statistics—the National Bureau of Economic Research—we did have a recession from March 2001 to November 2001. But last week, the Commerce Department released revised statistics that cast doubt on how severe the economic slowdown was during that period.

One rule of thumb says a recession occurs when GDP declines for two consecutive quarters. Prior to the revised numbers, GDP declined for the first three quarters of 2001 and easily fit the rule-of-thumb definition for a recession. However, the revised numbers show GDP declined in the first quarter of 2001, rose in the second quarter, and then declined in the third quarter. That pattern no longer fits the rule-of-thumb definition.

Whether or not we "officially" had a recession in 2001 is really a moot point though. It's only relevant to economists and politicians. For the rest of us, the key is to try and make sure the next national recession does not turn into a personal recession for us. We'll try to help you avoid such an outcome through effective financial planning.

Being a successful investor requires that we learn from the past. We've all made investment mistakes over the years, but the most successful investors are those who learn from their mistakes, make adjustments, and keep moving forward. Otherwise, as philosopher George Santayana said, "Those who cannot remember the past are condemned to repeat it."

Here are six of the mistakes I've seen investors make over the years that may be corrected by "remembering the past."

1. No investment strategy. Success requires a well-planned strategy that incorporates your time horizon, your ability to handle volatility, and your goals.
2. Acting on tips and hunches. Success requires analysis and investigation to determine which investments are right for you.
3. Lack of diversification. Success requires a diversified portfolio that can help you hit singles and doubles instead of swinging for the fences. Hunting for homers frequently leads to striking out.
4. Always following the crowd. Success requires charting your own path, which may or may not involve following the crowd. Remember the "herd mentality" I mentioned earlier.
5. Constant trading. Success requires thinking long term. If you take the time to make good buy decisions, you shouldn't have to trade too frequently.
6. Unrealistic expectations. Success requires a thorough understanding of the history of capital markets. Although past performance is no guarantee of future results, knowing what took place in the past can help us frame our expectations for the future.

By avoiding these six mistakes, I believe you'll have a much better chance to successfully reach your investment goals.

FIGURE 12.1 *Sample Commentary, continued*

Weekly Focus—The State of Giving in America

According to a June 2004 study by the Giving USA Foundation, American individuals, estates, foundations, and corporations gave an estimated $241 billion to charitable causes in 2003. That's an increase of 2.8 percent over 2002. As a percentage of GDP, charitable giving in 2003 comes out to about 2.2 percent, which is just shy of the all-time record of 2.3 percent of GDP in 2000. Since 1998, charitable giving has been at 2.0 percent of GDP or higher. Prior to 1998, charitable giving was below 2.0 percent for more than 20 years. So it appears there's an uptrend in giving over the past few years.

Economists seem baffled by the trend. They have a hard time explaining logically why people would work hard all their life only to turn around and give it away. As they say in economics, it's just not "rational."

Being rational may help when it comes to investing, but when it comes to giving, a little "irrationality" doesn't hurt.

Best regards,

Carson Wealth Management Group

The only problem with the market commentary idea is that it requires a significant time commitment. It's written every week, and it's written over the weekend. To alleviate this problem, we make our commentary available to all financial advisors who are members of the Peak Productions coaching program. Coaching members receive the commentary on a ghost-written basis and thus allows them to put their name on it.

2. Birthday Call

One of the activities with the highest value and lowest cost you can perform in your practice is calling your clients on their birthday. It takes no more than a few minutes a day, yet the reaction we've received from our clients has been phenomenal. We've had clients tell us that their grandchildren don't even call them on their birthday. Others have told us that the one thing they can count on in life is receiving a call on their birthday from Carson Wealth Management Group. But here's one caveat—don't start calling your clients on their birthday until you're 100 percent confident you will continue it indefinitely. One of the worst things you can do is elevate your level of service, get your clients used to it, and then pull the rug out from under them and drop it back down. Once you set an expectation, you have to maintain it.

The birthday call is even more powerful when the birthday falls on a weekend. That's right, don't wait until Monday to call, pick up the phone on Saturday or Sunday, and make the call. Don't forget that this is a birthday call, not a business call. If the client wants to talk business, say, "Mary, I was calling just to wish you a Happy Birthday. If you want to talk business, we need to hang up and I'll call you back." Your intention is so important here. You're not making the calls to drum up more business. You're making the calls because you genuinely care about your clients.

You should develop a formal system for making birthday calls. Most contact management systems can track birthdays, so your job is to figure out how to translate the birthday information into actually making the calls. If one of your staff members needs to run a report each week/month and hand it to you, that's fine. If you have a contact management system that automatically schedules the birthday calls on your calendar, that's great. The point is, develop a system and make the calls. As the advisor, you should make the calls to your A+ and A clients, and another team member can make the calls to your B clients. If you have a mobile phone, program it with your A+ and A clients' phone numbers and then call them on their birthday as you make your way home from the office. For an added touch, call your clients on their wedding anniversary too.

The birthday call is powerful, takes very little time, and not only makes your clients feel great makes you feel great too. Make it a part of your day.

3. Client Events

About ten times each year, we invite our clients to get together for an event that helps us deepen the relationship. These events fall into three categories. First, they could be purely educational, such as bringing in a portfolio manager or other industry speaker. Second, they could be purely entertainment, such as our annual Fourth of July dinner and fireworks show. Or, third, they could be "edutainment," a combination of both, such as our annual Half-time Report and Wine Social. We'll talk about client events in detail later in the book, but suffice it to say they're a great way to communicate with a large number of your clients in a positive way.

4. Proactive Touch-base Calls

When Alexander Graham Bell invented the telephone more than 100 years ago, who would have thought how indispensable it would become? We've already discussed birthday calls and anniversary calls. Now we'd like you to add monthly and quarterly proactive touch-base calls. These calls are designed to simply check in with your clients, make sure everything's going well, and solve any problems before they get out of control. Occasionally, your client will say, "I'm glad you called,; I've got some additional money I want to do something with." In addition, when market circumstances warrant, you can use these calls to discuss timely events such as the recent mutual fund scandal.

We call our A+ clients every month and our A and B clients every quarter. Making these calls is so important that we tie it into our team goals, and the staff is given bonuses for making them. You should make the calls to your A+ clients, but your Love Affair Marketing person can call the A and B clients. Regardless of who makes the calls, they need to be tracked, and details of the conversations must be noted in your contact management system.

5. Client Newsletter

Sending a periodic client newsletter (quarterly or semiannually) is a great way to let your individuality shine through and add to the total experience your clients receive from doing business with you. There are numerous third-party vendors offering newsletter services, but we encourage you to develop your own, which reflects your personality and uniqueness. Here are a few items you may want to incorporate into your newsletter:

* *Educational articles.* Obviously, you'll want to publish articles that are timely and relevant to your readers. These should be written in-house or you can utilize a third-party ghostwriting service that specializes in our industry.
* *Articles of interest.* A newsletter filled with industry articles is boring. Sprinkle in some other articles, stories, or anecdotes that are not industry related. This is one area where you can let your personality shine. For example, here's a short story we've used.

America's First Road Trip

It all started 100 years ago when Horatio Nelson Jackson bet $50 that he could drive a car from San Francisco to New York City in less than three months. Now keep in mind that back in 1903, there was no Lincoln Highway, no gas stations, and only 150 miles of paved roads in all of America, according to Dayton Duncan, author of *Horatio's Drive: America's First Road Trip.* Undaunted, Jackson spent $3,000 to buy a Winton touring car, bought some spare equipment, and hired a mechanic. Within four days they were on the road.

The first day didn't start too well. They got a flat tire and only traveled 83 miles in five hours on the road. Each succeeding day brought its shares of trials and tribulations from equipment failures to wrong turns to running out of gas. But as Jackson and his mechanic made their way across the country, their buzz grew (thanks to the telegraph) and "By the time they pulled into New York City on July 26—63 days after leaving San Francisco—they were a national sensation," according to Duncan.

Jackson's $50 bet ended up costing him $8,000 in expenses, but the notoriety was priceless. His cross-country road trip spawned a tradition of "roadtripping" that continues to this day.

You can find ideas for stories by scanning the Internet, perusing magazines, or by simply being observant and turning your everyday experiences into interesting copy.

- *Personal notes.* One of the most popular sections in our newsletter is personal notes. This is where each of our staff members writes a paragraph about whatever it is he or she would like to share with the rest of the world. The staff members can write about what's going on in their life, what trip they were just on, or what they're looking forward to. The personal notes humanize our staff members and help our clients better connect with us. At a recent Advisory Council meeting, our members said this is the first section (and sometimes the only section) they read.
- *Calendar of events.* Every issue should contain a list of your planned events with dates, times, and locations.
- *Whom to call.* Your efficiency and quality of life improves significantly if you train your clients to call your staff instead of you for all the little things. The "who-to-call" list should detail each staff member, the member's direct dial number, a brief description of the member's job along with the types of questions he or she answers, and, ideally, a headshot photo.

6. Articles of Interest

With all the reading you do, you're bound to come across an article that your clients would find interesting. When you do, get it approved through Compliance and then send it to your clients who you think would find it interesting. It doesn't even have to be about business. Maybe you have a handful of clients who love cars, and you read a great article in *Car and Driver* magazine. Get it approved, write a short note, and then drop it in the mail. You'll get lots of mileage out of this personal touch.

7. Holiday Letter

Many advisors send holiday cards during Christmas and New Year's. Going forward, consider sending a personal letter and family picture with your holiday card. The letter should be heartfelt and discuss some of the highlights of the past year, what you're looking forward to next year, and what you're thankful for. It helps your clients know you better from a personal standpoint and deepens your connection with them.

One thing's for sure: our clients never forget us because we stay top of mind. Look at your practice and count how many times each year you're communicating with clients. Is it less than 10? More than 20? Is your communication effective and coherent or just annoying? Take a hard look at the frequency of your communication and the messages you're sending to make sure they all add up to the impression you're hoping to generate.

An added benefit of all this communication is that we only have to personally meet with our clients once a year. They hear from us in so many other ways that we only need to have a one-on-one meeting on an annual basis. Many advisors are meeting with clients on a quarterly or semiannual basis, but that's not necessary when you have other communication mechanisms in place. If you're currently meeting with clients two to four times a year, imagine how much more time you'll have by implementing the communication systems we've just described and reducing your in-person meetings to once a year.

CLIENT SURVEY

Part of the communication process involves receiving feedback—both positive and negative—from our clients through a weekly drip-mail system. By the end of the year, all clients will have received a survey. We do this weekly instead of all at once so we can get continuous feedback throughout the year.

We review the questions on the survey each year at our annual staff retreat. It's a good idea to change it a little to keep your clients interested in filling it out. If they answer the same questions year after year, it becomes tedious. Our survey contains both a quantitative and qualitative section. We want to know numerically and subjectively if we are getting better. Here are four sample quantitative questions:

On a scale of 1 to 10 (1 being low and 10 being high) please rate the following.

1. Does our team promptly return your
   phone calls?   Rating: ___
   How important is this to you?   Rating: ___

2. Are your questions answered to your
   satisfaction by our team?   Rating: ___
   How important is this to you?   Rating: ___

3. Are the annual updates you receive
   from us easy to read and understand?   Rating: ___
   How important is this to you?   Rating: ___

4. How would you rate your overall level of
   service from Carson Wealth?   Rating: ____
   How important is this to you?   Rating: ____

Notice that after each question we ask, "How important is this to you?" The reason is that we want to make sure our allocation of resources is proper. For example, let's say a client gave us a 10 on the "Does our team promptly return your phone calls?" question but only a 5 on "How important is that to you?" Then let's say we drop down to the next question, "Are your questions answered to your satisfaction by our team?" and they rate that a 5, but in terms of importance they rate it a 10. This information would tell us we need to spend more time training and answering questions because that's more important to our clients than getting back to them promptly. We want to make sure we allocate our time to the areas that are most important to our clients.

The fifth question in our survey ties into our mission. We want to provide the best service possible, so we ask them directly:

5. Our goal is to provide you with the best service you have
   ever experienced.
   Are we currently doing that? _____ Yes _____ No
   If you answered no, what can we do to improve? _____
   _____

The average score for question 4 is calculated, and then we tie that into our staff's bonus compensation. If question 5 is answered Yes, we add one bonus point. To receive the quarterly bonus as it relates to customer service, the score has to average 10 or higher for the quarter. If we receive a 7 or below on question five, we call the client and specifically ask what we can do to improve.

We also ask a couple of qualitative questions such as these:

1. Is there anything you would like us to change or improve?

2. What do you think differentiates Carson Wealth Management Group from other financial planning firms you've worked with?

And, of course, we never miss an opportunity to ask for referrals, so we provide space on the survey for writing down names. As an added bonus to complete the surveys, each quarter we draw one name from the list of those who have completed surveys and send the winner a small gift.

ADVISORY COUNCIL

An effective, yet seldom used, communication idea is to set up an Advisory Council with your top clients. These clients represent a treasure trove of wisdom and experience, yet many advisors go no further than simply asking their top clients for referrals.

An Advisory Council is a small group of top clients who meet periodically in an effort to help you improve your business. These are clients who have a sincere interest in helping you grow and who enjoy being a sounding board, mentor, and referral source.

As you well know, corporations have a board of directors that is responsible for safeguarding and ensuring shareholders' assets. The board also provides input and guidance in managing the company and helps make major decisions. An Advisory Council is similar and provides you with all the benefits of a corporate board of directors. However, with an Advisory Council you avoid the major drawback of a corporate board of directors—ceding control to outsiders. You're in charge of your Advisory Council and can determine its makeup, agenda, and direction.

An Advisory Council can help you in several ways. First, you'll find that previously closed doors begin to open. Your top clients have lots of connections, and they can help you get into places you couldn't get into on your own. Second, you'll start receiving more referrals. As your top clients get to know you better, they'll feel more comfortable sharing names and more connected in helping you be successful. And third, your council will become a valuable medium for exchanging ideas and testing them before you make a mistake or spend money in an area that's not going to give you results.

The benefits to having an Advisory Council can be substantial. For Ron, he gained access to a Fortune 500 company and spoke during a brown-bag luncheon all because one of his council members made it happen. He had been trying on his own for months with no success. Another council member sent a referral that resulted in a $1 million rollover just two weeks after Ron's inaugural council meeting.

Your council can also save you possible embarrassment. Ron asked his council if they thought it would be a great idea to have a Salvation Army kettle at one of the Carson Wealth client events. The council shot it down. They felt it would be inappropriate and that guests might feel pressured to make a contribution.

Who should be on your Advisory Council? You'll want to start with the people you would like to clone—that is, your A+ clients and major centers of influence. You could even consider having an A+ prospect on your council, but that may slightly change the dynamics of the meeting. In any event, don't be afraid to ask your A+ clients to take half a day out of their busy schedule. You'll likely find that they were flattered you asked and are eager to help.

You won't be the only one to benefit from council meetings. Our clients have told us they get just as much out of the meetings as they give. For example, we've had several small business owners on our council who said they've implemented some of the customer service ideas they learned from us.

Here are a few thoughts from Ron that you should keep in mind as you consider establishing your own Advisory Council:

First, limit the size to about six to eight members. This is large enough to give you a good cross-section of your clients yet small enough to ensure a healthy dialogue.

Second, consider limiting your council members to a 24-month term. This ensures that you'll have a continual stream of new members who bring fresh perspectives and additional referral opportunities. It also allows you to get even more of your top clients involved.

Third, make sure you have a diverse mix of members. Your council might include men and women; a mix of young and old entrepreneurs; corporate executives; dot-com winners, or wealthy retirees. Your council members should represent the type of client you want to clone. As a side benefit, it is exciting to see the interplay among your highly successful clients who come from different backgrounds and perhaps different generations.

And fourth, make your key employees members of the council. There's a bundle of creativity inside them that will come out once they're in the electric atmosphere of your council meetings.

As with any good meeting, it's important to establish ground rules. First, let the council members know that every idea and every comment is valid. Second, ensure privacy by emphatically stating that what is said in the meeting stays in the meeting. And, third, let them know there are no taboo topics. The "no taboo topics" rule is the most important. Tell your council you want them to be brutally honest because it's their feedback that will help you get better.

Because you'll want to foster camaraderie and open dialogue among your members, consider starting each half-day meeting with a casual lunch and end with cocktails and dinner. This helps everyone loosen up and feel more comfortable around each other. It's also a good idea to start your first meeting by spending time sharing information about each other and getting to know each other on a more personal level.

Your meetings don't have to be expensive to be first-class. If you have a plush office, hold the meetings there; otherwise, move to a local country club or other classy location. Meeting twice a year for the first few years is a good target to shoot for. After that, you can meet once a year.

Before each meeting, send your members the agenda and give them some prep work. This will start them thinking about the topics ahead of time so they can come better prepared. Here are six agenda ideas you'll want to consider:

1. Review your mission and vision statements. Ask your members if these statements express the strength, dedication, and clarity of a company they want to do business with.

2. What makes your firm unique? You'll get some great (and possibly even surprising) feedback on why your top clients choose to do business with you.

3. Brainstorm for creative ideas. Your council can be really helpful here. Discuss ways you can lower costs, improve service, and enhance communication. For example, your council might suggest that to lower costs you should stop mailing your client surveys, and instead have each client complete them when they come in for a review. To improve communication, they might ask you to e-mail them a brief description of any asset allocation changes you make and why you made them. Our council told us we should change our client newsletter by shortening it, adding call-out boxes for important information, and giving clients the option to receive it by e-mail. That's great feedback.

4. Review next year's proposed client events. This discussion helps you determine if your events are on the mark. For example, we added a wine-tasting event as a result of feedback

from one of our Advisory Council meetings, and it turned out to be a big hit.

5. How can you grow your business? This is where you let the members know you are looking for more people just like them. You'll be surprised what comes out of the woodwork. Also, ask if there are opportunities for you to speak in front of groups they're affiliated with—company retirement groups, civic groups, or even brown-bag lunches.

6. Review your existing service offerings. At one of our council meetings we discovered that three of the council members did not know Carson Wealth offered tax services. As a result, a Carson Wealth staff member now calls all of the A+, A, and B clients whenever we add a new service. In addition, this prompted us to add a "services offered" section to the semiannual client newsletter.

At the end of your meetings, carve out 15 to 20 minutes for summarizing what was talked about. Then develop an action plan with timelines and communicate the progress through periodic e-mails. At the next meeting, close the loop by reviewing the status of each item.

Conclude your meetings by thanking the members, giving them each a small gift, and then adjourning for cocktails and dinner. A great idea for a small gift for new members would be a leather-bound portfolio with their initials embossed on it along with a nice pen.

Creating an Advisory Council is a proven strategy that benefits all involved. You benefit by having a sounding board for new ideas, a source for new referrals, and a partner in helping you develop a more effective and profitable business. Your clients benefit by picking up a few new ideas and by having a direct impact on the quality and types of services that you deliver to them. And together you benefit from the enhanced fellowship and camaraderie.

SUMMARY

- Building relationships and communicating with your clients and prospects is critical to distinguishing your business in the marketplace.
- Developing a trusting, connective relationship with your clients involves being genuine and sincere and asking good questions. You have to get to the heart of who they are and understand how you can help them achieve their hopes, dreams, and aspirations.
- Once you've established the relationship, you can continue to enhance it by communicating on a frequent basis through a variety of means. Frequent, effective communication keeps you top of mind, enhances your credibility, and deepens the relationship.
- The left half of the brain is the linear and logical side; the right half of the brain is the emotional and creative side. To truly connect with a prospect, you have to meet the needs of both sides of the brain. Stories are your path to do that, so practice your storytelling skills.

TNT #6 ACTION STEPS

- Develop a list of questions for you to ask during the client interview process. Use the 15 questions identified in this chapter as your starting point.

- Work on creating a few stories that communicate your value, that deepen the relationship, and that help turn complex ideas into easily understood concepts. Read *The Story Factor* by Annette Simmons.

- Implement a client and prospect communication strategy. Consider adding a weekly e-mail commentary, making birthday calls, delivering client events, making proactive touchbase calls, sending an in-house-created client newsletter, sending periodic articles of interest, and sending a holiday letter.

- Create a client satisfaction survey and send a few out each week. Score the results and tie the score into your staff's team bonus.

- Create an Advisory Council with your top clients.

FOCUS MARKETING EFFORTS ON TOP CLIENTS AND PROSPECTS

13

GET THE MOST
FROM YOUR MARKETING

"We expand what we focus on."
—WAYNE W. DYER

In 1967, Harvard psychologist Stanley Milgram sent a letter to a random sample of residents in Omaha. The letter contained the name of a Boston stockbroker along with his rough location and asked the Omaha residents to forward the letter to someone they thought could get the letter closer to the stockbroker. Milgram's objective was to see how many times the letter was forwarded before it reached the Boston stockbroker. Contrary to initial expectations, it took on average only five to seven "forwards" to get the letter to the stockbroker.

This simple experiment in the science of social networks gave rise to the concept of "six degrees of separation." Careful application of this concept could go a long way toward doubling or tripling your business. The key is to grow your business through people you know, and we're not just talking about simple networking here. We're talking about developing an intelligent plan to leverage your best relationships and connect with other high-net-worth individuals.

Let's put this idea to a test. Think of the president of the United States. How far removed are you from that person? We'll bet you only have to go through three or four people at most before you could be connected. And if that's the case with the president, imagine how close you are to the key prospects in your town. That's the concept and here's how you can execute it.

SERVICING YOUR CLIENTS

Your top clients are your best source for new top clients, so the first step is to make sure you're "showing the love" to them. Because there aren't enough hours in the day to treat every client the same, you have to distinguish the level of service you provide among clients, but you must be very careful how you do this. You don't want to provide great service to your best clients and then totally forget everybody else. If you do that, word will get around, and your reputation and brand will be shot. Instead, lavish the love on your best clients and use systems to keep your average clients happy.

As a reminder, here are a few ways to lavish the love. First, make a proactive call to your A+ clients every month and a quarterly proactive call to your A and B clients. Second, if you have a special event or a vacation home, make them available to your best clients. Third, if you're sending birthday gifts, make the gifts for your top clients a little nicer than for your average clients. Fourth, make the effort to write your top clients an occasional personal note on whatever topic strikes you. And, fifth, do random acts of kindness more frequently for your top clients.

Your top clients will notice these little extras and they'll help keep you top of mind.

THE A+ ACTION PLAN

Now that you know who your top clients are, you can significantly jump-start your practice by implementing the A+ Action Plan. This plan leverages your top relationships and introduces you to new high-net-worth individuals. Even if you have only one or two A+ clients, that's okay; you've got to start somewhere.

Here's the plan. From your existing list of A+ clients, add all warm A+ prospects plus all your old A+ prospects who "got away." Now individually take each one of the people on this list to breakfast, lunch, or dinner. Notice you're not meeting them at your office. The point is to move to a less formal environment where you and your guest can really bond.

Throughout the meeting, learn everything you possibly can about your guests so you can use it in your Love Affair Marketing program. What hobbies do they have? Where did they go to school? Do they have any pets? How did they meet their spouse? Who are their favorite sports teams? What are their hopes, dreams, and aspirations? You can also use this time to set up a future activity. For example, if you and a guest both enjoy golfing, set up a time and a place to golf and ask the guest to invite two of his or her colleagues that the guest would like to introduce to your firm. If you both like to play tennis, set up a doubles match. These events are designed to (1) have fun, (2) deepen the relationship, and (3) introduce you to new prospects.

After you've learned about the clients, it's your turn to open up and let your clients know that you're making some big changes in your practice. Tell them about your mission and vision. Let them know about all the changes you're making in your office and how you are putting systems and organization in place to dramatically elevate the level of service you provide. Explain that you want to grow, but you want to grow with the right kinds of clients who can benefit most from the services you provide. Tell them that for the benefit of your existing clients, you're only taking on a limited number of new clients each year. Talk about the changes our industry has gone through with the research scandal and the mutual fund scandal and how your firm is positioned to provide unbiased advice and work with best-of-breed products. Discuss the strategic alliances you've set up and how you can provide comprehensive wealth planning, including tax, estate, insurance, and investment planning, all coordinated by you with help from other specialized professionals.

Take as much time as you need and be totally honest, open, and sincere with them. You may even share with them the fact that you've had too many accounts in the past and that you're now bringing in an associate advisor to help manage them. This is the time to lay it all on the line.

Once you've made these comments, ask for feedback. Do they have any questions, comments, or ideas about how you can improve even more? By getting their feedback, they'll have more at stake in the success of your business and will feel more inclined to help you.

Close the meeting by asking for their help. Let them know that the best way they can help you is to refer people—just like themselves—to your firm. This part is absolutely critical, so don't skip it!

After the meeting, establish a top-of-mind awareness campaign. Now that you know what they like, you can send them an occasional article or Web site link to something they may find interesting. Perform a random act of kindness. The point is, be creative. Figure out ways to keep your name front and center with them.

The A+ Action Plan is one of the most effective, yet underutilized, ways to grow your practice. Skip it at your own risk.

REFERRAL MARKETING—THE MILLION-DOLLAR WAY™

Asking for a referral doesn't cost you any money. It doesn't require a PhD. All it requires is confidence in yourself that you deserve to have your top clients send referrals of people just like themselves. Unfortunately, many advisors get nervous just thinking about asking for a referral. Such thoughts as "My service isn't good enough to justify a referral" or "Her portfolio is still down from when she started working with me, so I can't ask her" to "He knows I want referrals, I don't have to ask" keep popping up and dissuading advisors from asking.

Well, if you want to be average, keep on being nervous.

Top producers cut through their fear and realize the worst thing a client can do when you ask for a referral is either say no or do nothing. Either way, it's not going to kill you. The downside to asking for a referral is limited, but the upside is the Executive Council.

Many of the advisors who do ask for a referral are stuck in the "Do you know anybody who could utilize my services?" school of referral marketing—a scattershot method that generates random results. A more effective method turns referral marketing into a system. This system uses a multipronged approach that has generated proven results for hundreds of the country's leading financial advisors.

By systematizing your referral marketing process, you'll enjoy several benefits.

First, you'll elevate the professionalism of asking for referrals. Many advisors don't ask for referrals because they feel uncomfortable. By systematizing the process, referral marketing becomes an activity with clearly defined steps, and this should improve your confidence and make the process much smoother.

Second, you'll develop a repeatable process for generating referrals that you can refine and improve over time. When you use a scattershot approach to asking for referrals, no two situations are the same. You don't know which approach worked and which one didn't, so you have no ability to refine and improve. By creating a system for asking for referrals, you use the same process every time and can expect similar results every time. If something's not working, you can simply tweak the process to improve your results.

Third, your clients will realize you're serious about referrals, and this will make them more willing to provide them. The old school method of referral marketing leaves clients unimpressed. They know they can easily ignore your request to pass out a few business cards or share some names of people who may be interested in your services. With Referral Marketing the Million-Dollar Way, your clients will clearly understand that not only do you want referrals but you expect them, and that's part of the "deal" of working with you.

And, fourth, you'll improve your quality of life. By enlisting your clients to help you market, you'll spend less time shaking the trees for new business and have more time for your existing clients and for yourself.

There are several steps in generating referrals the Million-Dollar Way.

The first step is to be careful whom you ask for a referral. If you ask a C client for a referral, you'll most likely get a C prospect in return. Clients tend to refer people who are in their same socioeconomic circle—rarely do they "refer up." Your A+ and A clients are the only clients for whom you should be implementing this million-dollar referral marketing system.

The second step is to make your clients aware that sending you referrals is part of your compensation. This means when you meet with a new client, you have to let that person know up front that you expect referrals. If people sign on with you, then they are effectively committing to sending referrals of people just like themselves.

Here's a script from Ron on how you could explain this during the beginning of the client relationship. Let's say Mr. and Mrs. Jones just asked how you are paid. You could launch into the following:

Mr. and Mrs. Jones, I have a unique way in which I collect my fee for service. The reason it's unique is that it allows us to work closely together to reach our common goals.

My goal is to help you reach your financial objectives. It's hard for me to do that if I have to spend a lot of my time prospecting for new business. I would much rather spend my time monitoring, reviewing, and developing solutions for my clients just like you.

As you will notice throughout our relationship, I have a very competent team of assistants who will help me take care of your every need. I delegate all the things I'm either not good at or where my time is not efficiently used.

So that brings me back to how I collect my fee for service for helping you.

I am very good at two things: making your money grow and monitoring your goals and objectives.

My goal is to spend 80 percent of my time doing these activities. If I'm out prospecting, I can't help you reach your goals. So I've had an agreement with my clients, which over the years has worked very well.

First, 50 percent of my compensation comes from a fee (or commission) for my service (explain your compensation).

Second, and most important, the other half of my compensation comes from referrals you send to me. I really need you to be on the lookout for people just like you who could benefit from our services. When the time is right, I would like you to send us someone just like yourself. We're going to have lots of different events throughout the year, and those are great times to invite one of your friends or colleagues to join us. It's a fun, nonthreatening environment.

At this point, Mr. and Mrs. Jones have a clear understanding that you expect referrals. However, they probably have no idea what a "good" referral looks like, and they probably don't know the appropriate time to make a referral. Very few people have ever been "trained" how to make referrals.

This leads us to step three of the system, which is to train your clients to be on the lookout for appropriate referral opportunities. You can do this by painting a picture for your clients of what type of prospect they should be looking for and in what kind of situation it would be appropriate to make a referral. Ron continues.

Mr. and Mrs. Jones, for the benefit of my existing clients, I accept only a limited number of new clients each year. So that you can feel comfortable referring people to our firm, I'd like to share with you the type of people who can benefit most from our services. The people we can help the most are those just like you who . . . (describe what your ideal client looks like in terms of net worth, complexity, demographics, etc.). Also, there are certain times when it may be appropriate to bring up [your firm's name] in the course of a conversation. For example, here are a few scenarios when it may be appropriate for you to mention us:

- One of your business colleagues is retiring and has a rollover.
- A friend's, colleague's, or relative's spouse just died.
- A friend, colleague, or relative is complaining about low interest rates.
- A friend, colleague, or relative just inherited money.
- A friend, colleague, or relative is complaining about poor service, performance, or communication from their existing advisor.
- You're out with your friends talking about the markets and retirement.

In order for this dialogue to work, you have to be serious about it. If you present this as an option more than a requirement, then fewer clients will respond. One reason why this works is that you're not putting the client on the spot to come up with a name. As a result, you get a steady flow of prospects who need your services at a particular time.

Step four of the system focuses on keeping the thought of referrals top of mind with your clients. This involves sending your clients quarterly referral letters and reminding them periodically that you expect referrals. You usually have several opportunities during the year to remind your clients that you expect referrals. For example, you can remind them during a review meeting. You can remind them in the invitations you send to your client events. And you can even mention it occasionally in any e-mail communication you may have. The key is your wanting clients to always be on the lookout for referral opportunities.

As you upgrade your referral marketing system, don't fall into the trap of rewarding your clients for giving referrals. Some advisors reward their clients with a wine glass for each referral and tell them that if they send eight referrals, they can get a whole set. The problem with this strategy is you'll end up attracting the wrong type of client—the type of client who expects a toaster on opening a CD. You want your clients to send referrals because they appreciate the quality of your service and advice—not because you reward them.

Nobody said this was going to be easy, but then again, getting to million-dollar production isn't easy either.

If you make the effort to follow this proven, four-step system to Generating Referrals the Million-Dollar Way, you'll end up spending less time on marketing, have more time to help your clients, increase your income, and improve your quality of life. That's a pretty good trade-off.

PASSION PROSPECTING™

Passion Prospecting is the third key strategy for building your business by leveraging your existing relationships. Historically, it's been drilled into our heads that to build your business you have to focus on a niche. Typically, we're told to focus on such niches as doctors or small business owners or divorcees because that's where the money is.

We think that advice is all wrong.

According to Ron:

I've found the best way to build your practice is to focus on what you're passionate about. Life is too short to spend time with people you don't enjoy or connect with. Instead, work with people who share the same passions and hobbies as you do.

Here's how it works. I have four passions outside of my family and my faith and they are golf, Nebraska football, fine red wine, and my newest passion, which is flying. Most of my new business comes from people I meet when I'm engaged in one of these four activities.

For example, when I play golf, I invite an A+ client and ask him or her to invite two friends or colleagues to round out the foursome. And you know what? Nine times out of ten those guests will be of the same socioeconomic status as my A+ client. By the time we play golf for four hours and have a drink on the 19th hole, we're all pretty good friends, and that leads effortlessly to "Well, tell me a little more about what you do, Ron."

Ten years ago, I was prospecting a high-net-worth individual, but he could never find time to meet with me for lunch or a quick 15-minute meeting. Fortunately, one of my A+ clients knew him and arranged for us to play together in a golf tournament. After spending almost the whole day with him (remember, this is the same person who did not have time for a 15-minute meeting), I casually asked him, "Who handles your money?" He said it was spread among several people, but he wouldn't mind getting together with me for lunch to discuss how we could help him.

We met for lunch and he's been a client for ten years.

By connecting with him through a common passion, I was able to spend nearly a whole day with him. When I approached him from a purely business angle, he couldn't find 15 minutes for me. People will always make time for their passion.

I've also hosted a chipping and putting clinic at my club. For a small fee I hired the club pro to give my group a few pointers, after which we set up a chipping and putting contest. We all had a great time, picked up a few ideas, and were able to converse in a relaxed setting that was conducive to relationship building.

It's the same thing with Nebraska football. I own a sky box at the stadium and on football Saturdays, I'm there with my A+ clients and my A+ prospects. It's such a positive, electric environment that developing a relationship happens naturally. Once the relationship is developed, taking the next step to working together is much easier.

To pursue my passion for drinking and collecting fine red wine, I joined the International Wine and Food Society. Recently, I invited several local chapter members to a dinner and wine-tasting event at a local restaurant. My only link to these people was our common interest in wine. I began the evening with a few introductory comments about my firm and the markets; then I turned the evening over to a local wine expert, who gracefully led my guests through a series of wines that accompanied dinner.

Throughout the course of the evening, I said hello to each guest (there were 12) and engaged in the usual chitchat. One guest in particular shared several passions with me. He loved Nebraska football, so I invited him to attend a game and sit in my sky box. He wanted to improve his golf game, so I set him up with my instructor. And, of course, he loved wine.

Not surprisingly, this particular guest set up an appointment, and we discussed his situation. Turns out his money was scattered among several advisors. I described how we could consolidate his assets and provide comprehensive planning services. He said we were exactly what he was looking for. Two weeks later he transferred an $8.5 million account.

This is a perfect example of how Passion Prospecting works. We got to know each other over dinner and a glass of wine, found common ground, and then developed a business relationship.

Maybe your hobbies aren't the same as Ron's, but all of us have hobbies that we enjoy outside the office. It could be boating, tennis, or going to the symphony. Whatever they are, think creatively how you can set up events that center around your passions. Then invite your clients who share that passion, ask them to bring a friend or colleague, bond with them, and let your natural instincts take over when it comes to figuring out the right time to bring up business.

If the prospect takes the initiative and asks you what you do for a living, be prepared. Have a very short but intriguing answer that begs for a follow-up. For example, you might say, "I'm in the proactive wealth management business." Unless the prospect is brain dead, the response is "What does that mean?" Now you can start a dialogue that should end with an agreement to meet in your office.

There's one requirement, however, you have to meet for Passion Prospecting to work—you must be above average in your passion. For example, if it's golf, you should shoot in the 80s or better. If it's tennis, you shouldn't be making too many unforced errors. If it's wine, you ought to know that "bouquet" is not a bunch of flowers. If you're passionate about something but not yet above average in your skill or knowledge, brush up before you start participating in it with prospects and clients.

To start your own Passion Prospecting, simply follow these three steps.

1. Figure out what you're passionate about.
2. Develop events around your passion.
3. Subtly tie your business into each event with the goal of making an appointment.

Billionaire Richard Branson summed it up nicely when he said, "I don't view work as work and play as play; it's all living." Passion Prospecting is a seamless and enjoyable way to mix business and pleasure. It has allowed Ron to significantly increase his income and at the same time enhance his quality of life. It can do the same for you.

SUMMARY

- The science of social networks is very instructive when it comes to building your business. Studies have shown that even though there are more than 300 million people in North America, we're just a few relationships away from knowing virtually every one of them. That's a powerful concept, and it leads directly to the idea that you should grow your business by leveraging your key relationships.
- Your top clients are your best source for new top clients, so you have to make sure you take good care of them. Because there are not enough hours in the day to treat every client the same, you need to distinguish the level of service you provide, but you have to be very careful how you do this. You don't want to provide great service to your best clients and then totally forget everybody else.

- The A+ Action Plan is one of the most effective, yet under-utilized, ways to grow your practice.
- Referral Marketing the Million-Dollar Way doesn't cost you any money. It doesn't require a PhD. All it requires is confidence in yourself that you deserve to have your top clients send referrals of people just like themselves.
- Passion Prospecting is one of the most enjoyable ways to grow your business and improve your quality of life.

TNT #7 ACTION STEPS

- Segment your clients into A+, A, B, C, and D. Fire the D clients.

- Start distinguishing the level of service you provide to your clients. Make a proactive call to your A+ clients every month and a quarterly proactive call to your A and B clients. If you host a special event or own a vacation home, make it available to your best clients. If you're sending birthday gifts, make the gifts for your top clients a little nicer than those for your average clients. Make the effort to write your top clients an occasional personal note on whatever topic strikes you. Perform random acts of kindness more frequently for your top clients.

- Implement the A+ Action Plan.

- Implement the Referral Marketing the Million-Dollar Way system.

- Implement Passion Prospecting.

DELIVER
CLIENT EVENTS

14

DEEPEN RELATIONSHIPS
AND HAVE FUN DOING IT

*"In every instance, we found that the best-run companies stay as close
to their customers as humanly possible."*

—TOM PETERS

Would you rather spend $6,000 on a dinner seminar with 50 prospects—most of whom are there just for the free dinner—or invest that $6,000 in deepening your relationship with your top clients?

One of the biggest ironies in our business is that advisors will spend thousands of dollars on total strangers instead of investing that same amount of money in their current clients. It's really pretty crazy when you think about it. Imagine this scenario. You send out 8,000 mail pieces along with a ticket that entitles the recipient to a free sit-down dinner at your local country club. You give a value-added presentation and everyone's happy . . . except for your clients who aren't invited. The next day one of your top clients calls you and says, "John, I was just talking to my neighbor, and he said you bought him dinner last night and gave him a free presentation on *Six Ways to Reduce Your Taxes;* why haven't you ever taken me out to dinner?"

Uh oh.

Public seminars have their place and can be effective in the right circumstance. The right circumstance would be when an advisor has not yet built up a significant client base. In this case, public workshops (we prefer the name workshop over seminar) can be an effective way to increase your visibility and help build your business. For advisors in this situation, Peak Productions offers a turnkey public workshop that has been used very successfully by advisors all over the country.

For more established advisors, we recommend that you redirect part of your marketing budget to your existing clients and show them some extra "love" rather than spend all of your budget on trying to woo strangers. This will make you feel better because you'll be spending more time with people you know and care about. It will also lead to more business because your existing clients will gradually turn over more assets for you to manage, and they'll bring their friends and colleagues to the events that in turn will lead to more warm referrals.

What we're talking about here are *client events*. Instead of inviting total strangers to a public workshop, invite your clients to a specific event that could be educational, entertaining, or a combination of both. Then encourage your clients to bring a guest that they'd like to introduce to your firm.

These events accomplish three goals.

1. You become and stay top of mind with your clients and prospects.
2. You deepen your existing client relationships.
3. You create an outlet for clients to refer prospects to you in a nonthreatening way.

The educational events add to your credibility and give you an opportunity to reach a large number of your clients at one time. As an added benefit, this increases your free time because it reduces the number of times you have to meet with them individually. The entertainment events help deepen your relationship. And the "edutainment" events accomplish both. Let's take a look at how Ron's client events have evolved over the years, beginning with the first one in 1989.

Just imagine this. It's a true story. I couldn't make it up if I tried. I decided to have my first event in a steak house. Now you would think I'd have the common sense to ask the steak house if there were a room where we could be away from everybody else, right? Well, that wasn't the case.

It was a huge steak house, and I didn't check it out beforehand. Turns out they have all these seats and the tables set up, but they're set up right in the middle of the restaurant. So not only is it noisy, but my guest panel was right in the middle of it too. My first speaker was my accountant who was going to talk about living trusts. I had asked him ahead of time if he could talk about living trusts, and he said sure. Unfortunately, I never bothered to ask him if he knew anything about living trusts. He was so bad, I was embarrassed. I knew nothing about living trusts, but I at least knew a little more than he did.

Then I had a Medicare supplement salesperson come up and talk about Medicare supplements. And he was even worse than the accountant talking about living trusts. To top it all off, I had a wholesaler who was new to the business give a talk about the stock market. Not only was he clueless about the market, but he had stage fright and clammed up. So that was my first event. And believe it or not, clients had a good time. They were there in the middle of this big restaurant; it was noisy and just hilarious. Despite that inauspicious start, I continue to do client events to this day.

Even though Ron thought the event was a disaster, the 300 attendees actually loved it. The following year, this annual client

appreciation event moved to a local hotel banquet room. Here's
how the size of the event grew those first few years:

Year	Guests
1990	450
1991	500
1992	750
1993	1,000
1994	1,400
1995	1,600+
1996	New Program

By 1996, the event had outgrown the largest banquet facility
in town, and that's when Ron decided to totally revamp it. With
more than 1,600 people at one event, there was no way he could
greet everybody. It was just out of control because many of the attendees were kids and other assorted people who never had any
hope of becoming clients. They were just there for the free prime
rib. So Ron decided to deliver a series of smaller events throughout the year that would be a little more personal and allow him to
spend more time deepening relationships.

To figure out what types of events to hold, he surveyed his
clients and discovered that they seemed to enjoy dancing, garden-
ing, and golfing. So in the next couple years he added these types
of events to his mix.

The problem was that Ron had no interest in dancing or gar-
dening so participating in those events became more of a chore.
He did like golfing so that's when he decided to start offering
events that catered more to his interests. The theory was that by
doing events he enjoyed, he'd attract other people with similar
interests, and that would make it much easier to deepen the relationship with existing clients and start relationships with new
prospects.

CLIENT EVENT IDEAS

Here are some of the more recent events held by Carson Wealth Management Group.

2001

February	Where Do We Go from Here? (Ron: market update)
March	Rational Investing in an Irrational World (Ron)
April	Surviving This Bipolar Market (Ron)
May	Presentation by Portfolio Manager
July	Golf Event with Arnold Palmer, Gary Player, Lee Trevino and Chi Chi Rodriquez (sponsored by local country club)
July	Halftime Report (Ron: midyear market update)
September	Presentation on Oil and Gas (sponsor)
October	Presentation from Chief Investment Strategist at a Fund Company
October	Tailgate Party for Nebraska Football Game
December	Holiday Brunch

2002

January	Educational Presentation on 10 Ways to Wealth (Ron)
February	Valentine's Day Luncheon
April	Presentation from Chief Economist at a Fund Company
May	Charity Wine Social
June	Fireworks Show (sponsored by local country club)
July	Swing for Charity (golf outing)
July	Halftime Report (Ron: midyear market update)
August	Presentation by Portfolio Manager
August	Short Game School (golf outing)
September	Charity Wine Tasting
December	Holiday Brunch

2003

January	Questions to Ask Aging Parents Workshop (Ron)
February	The Top 7 Indicators of a Market Recovery Workshop (Ron)
April	Real Estate Workshop (sponsor)
May	Charity Wine Social

(continued)

June	Presentation by Chief Economist at a Fund Company
June	Fireworks Show (sponsored by local country club)
July	Halftime Report (Ron: midyear market update)
July	Alaskan Cruise
August	Short Game School
August	Swing for Charity (golf outing)
December	Holiday Brunch

2004

February	Presentation by Chief Investment Strategist
March–May	Health Challenge
June	Fireworks Show (sponsored by local country club)
July	Halftime Report (Ron: midyear market update)
August	Swing for Charity (golf outing)
October	An Evening with the Presidents (comedian)
December	Holiday Brunch

As you can see, some events have become a tradition and are repeated each year. Other events are onetime only and take advantage of what's going on at that time. We do about 8 to 12 events a year, and we have one person whose primary responsibility is to coordinate these events. You may not be in a position yet to do this many events, but at a minimum you should start with 4 events. Your first one could be an educational event in February or March to discuss how the year is setting up. That could be followed during the summer with some type of entertainment event that takes advantage of your personal interests (e.g., baseball game, fireworks show, golf outing). Late July is a great time to do a halftime report for discussing how the year is progressing; and you could end that event with some type of social activity such as a wine tasting. Consider finishing the year with a holiday brunch in early December.

GENERAL RULES ON HOSTING CLIENT EVENTS

Here are 12 general rules for hosting client events:

1. Always ask for permission to send an information packet to a prospect who attends your event. As a courtesy, if one of your clients brought the prospect, also ask the client if it's okay.

2. When applicable, try to host your events at a country club instead of a hotel. Country clubs are much nicer settings and have a tendency to attract a higher-net-worth clientele. If you don't golf or play tennis, you can still get a social membership and use the facility for your events and dinners.

3. Be creative when you're coming up with ideas for events. One advisor we work with rented a bus and took a group of his clients and prospects on a tour of holiday lights. Another advisor in Connecticut takes his clients on a boat trip down a river to view the fall foliage. Take advantage of what's going on in your own backyard by piggybacking on things that are already happening. For example, a charity may bring a speaker or celebrity into town, and you can attach yourself to that event and purchase a few inexpensive tickets.

4. Always be entertaining. Who are some of the highest-paid people in the country? Entertainers! So even though you're talking about serious issues, throw some levity into your events—it will make the medicine go down a little easier. Give away prizes. Always take a bunch of small gifts to these events, whether it's bottles of wine, golf balls, or shirts. People who are worth millions of dollars still love winning things.

5. Have a detailed system for putting on events. Create a checklist for every activity that has to take place and fol-

low it. Your events will go much more smoothly, and you'll be much more efficient. Here are several system ideas:

- Always set the room for 85 percent of the confirmed reservations. It will look a lot better if you have to bring in two or three chairs versus having a lot of empty ones.
- Colorcode your name tags. Use one color for a client and a different color for a prospect. Also, put a little tick mark on the name tag if the individual is having a birthday. For example, if his or her birthday is coming up in the next 30 days, put a little tick mark in the upper right-hand corner of the name tag. If his or her birthday was in the last 30 days, put a little tick mark in the left-hand corner of the name tag. And if today happened to be his or her birthday, put a little dot right in the center of the name tag. It's details like this that will impress your clients.
- Always conduct meeting and speaker evaluations. Here are a few questions you may want to ask on your evaluation: How did you like the speaker? Was the speaker interesting? What can we do to improve? What other topics would you like to hear about?
- Always take notes during each meeting. Look at what went right and what went wrong. Use these notes to keep improving each event.

6. Have some events that cater specifically to your A+ clients. Perhaps it's a book signing with a chief investment strategist who has written his own book. Perhaps it's a charity wine event with a high suggested donation. The key is to do something special for these high-net-worth people that is above and beyond what everybody else gets.

7. Have a goal for each event. Tell your audience what you hope to accomplish by having the event so they know what to expect.

8. Send invitations about two weeks before the event. If you send them earlier than that, they'll forget. Of course, you should promote the events in your client newsletter so your clients can plan in advance, but save the personal invitations until a couple of weeks before the event.

9. Never push specific products. You should be client focused, not product focused.

10. Never start more than five minutes late. It's important to show respect for the people who showed up on time.

11. Never exclude B, C, or D clients from events. Even though you don't want more B, C, or D clients, you have to invite them because it's not their fault that they are lower rated. It's not their fault that you took them on as clients, so we feel you have an obligation to invite them. However, you can and should make an extra effort to invite your A+ and A clients through phone calls.

12. Never allow your events to last more than 90 minutes unless it's some type of social event like a golf outing. People have trouble paying attention for longer than about 90 minutes so be brief. As Steve's father-in-law told him, "The key to being a successful speaker is to stand up so you can be seen, speak up so you can be heard, and be brief so you can be appreciated."

SUMMARY

- Taking care of your existing clients instead of spending all your marketing dollars searching for new clients is an important aspect of building your business. One of the best ways to do that is to host client events.
- There are three types of client events:
  1. Educational events to build your credibility
  2. Entertainment events to deepen your relationship
  3. Edutainment events to do both

- Doing client events accomplishes three goals:
  1. You become and stay top of mind with your clients and prospects.
  2. You deepen your existing client relationships.
  3. You create an outlet for clients to refer prospects to you in a nonthreatening way.

TNT #8 ACTION STEPS

- Identify a person on your staff who can be responsible for coordinating client events.

- Create a client event system that details the timeline and every step necessary to put on the event.

- Develop a plan to deliver a minimum of 4 events over the next year. Gradually work your way up to 8 to 12 events a year. Plan on about one-third being educational, one-third social, and one-third a combination of both.

- Always have attendees complete an event evaluation, and use the feedback to improve your events.

FOLLOW THE HABITS
OF TOP ACHIEVERS

15

DO WHAT WORKS

"To accomplish great things, we must not only act, but also dream.
Not only plan, but also believe."

—ANATOLE FRANCE

What separates the top achievers from the average achievers?

Top achievers have simply cracked the code for success. In all other respects, they're the same. They live by the same 24-hour clock. They eat. They sleep. They work. They play. They make mistakes. So what is the code for success?

There are two ways to be successful in business. First, you can be a pioneer and invent something new or become the first person to do something a certain way. The odds of success are small, but the rewards can be great. Or, second, you can learn what other successful people have done and then follow in their footsteps. The odds of success here are much higher, and the rewards can be just as great.

As advisors, we want you to combine the best of both strategies. It's somewhat like the "core and satellite" approach to building a portfolio. You have a core position that will deliver predictable results and a satellite position that gives you the opportunity to hit the ball out of the solar system. As you build your practice, about

80 percent of your time should be spent in the core following the TNT strategies we've discussed in our book. The remaining 20 percent of your time should be spent pioneering—experimenting and figuring out new and improved ways to do things.

The code for success is really an overlay to the core and satellite approach described above. Ron calls this code "The 15 Habits of Top Achievers," and you should follow the habits to build your business and enhance your quality of life.

Ron cracked the code over a period of years after having met and studied top achievers from all walks of life. He noticed that many of them shared certain similar characteristics. These characteristics, or habits as Ron calls them, are defined as doing the appropriate activities on a consistent basis, and they define the code for success. Although not everybody exhibited each of these habits, Ron summarizes his findings about the characteristics of top achievers as follows:

1. **They have a Relentless Burning Desire to succeed.** I've always said that you can work smart, have discipline, and be knowledgeable, but if you don't have a burning desire to succeed, you'll never make it to million-dollar production. Unfortunately, burning desire is not something I or anybody else can give you. It comes from within. But what I and my team at Peak Productions can do is help you ignite it. The key is to find something you get excited about, dig deep, and then make a commitment to yourself and your family that you will no longer settle for mediocrity. If you do this, you'll be one giant step closer to million-dollar production.

2. **They have a guiding light.** Burning desire coupled with a written personal mission statement, a business mission statement, and a compelling vision for your future is the surest way to ensure your success going forward. And don't just make them words on paper. You have to live and

breathe your mission and vision and use them as your guiding light. Print them in color, laminate them at your local print shop, and put them in a place where you will see them every day. Begin the day with your mission and vision in mind, and you'll end the day one step closer to their realization.

3. **They have well defined short-term, medium, and long-term goals that meet the SMAC test—specific, measurable, achievable, compatible.** Clear goals allow you to stay focused on your mission and vision, allow you to measure your progress, and help keep you motivated during the difficult times. Like your mission and vision, you should laminate your goals and put them in a place where you will see them every day. To download a mission, vision, and goal-setting template, go to http://www.peakproductions.com.

4. **They always live by the motto "I must do the most productive thing at every given moment."** There are only so many hours in the day and losing a few minutes here and a few minutes there adds up. To stay focused and productive, implement this simple tested-in-the-trenches tip that we mentioned earlier. *End each day by writing down the six most important things you have to do the next day in order of priority and then follow that list in order.* It's deceivingly simple, yet very few people do it. I can assure you, if you practice this every day, your productivity and your profits will rise significantly.

5. **They plan their time well in advance.** If you don't schedule your day, week, and month, it's easy to get distracted and be interrupted. Keeping an updated calendar helps you avoid conflicts and be more efficient in allocating your time. And, by the way, top achievers schedule personal reflection time too.

6. **They are early risers.** By rising 30 minutes earlier than you usually do each day, you can add two weeks to your year.

Imagine what you can do in two extra weeks. You could spend more time with the people who are important to you. You could improve your health. You could broaden your horizon by reading. Early risers get a leg up on the competition and use this extra time to their advantage.

7. **They are health conscious.** Being a top achiever requires energy and stamina. Regular exercise and a healthy diet make you feel good, improve your confidence, and give you the fuel to keep going when everyone else is falling by the wayside.

8. **They know the difference between good fear and bad fear.** Good fear is the butterflies we get in our stomach before a speech or the nervousness before a big event. It's natural, and it helps raise our pulse so we'll be fully engaged and sharp. It's your ally. Bad fear is paralyzing. It's worrying about things you have no control over (like the markets). It's defeating and it zaps your confidence. Get rid of it.

9. **They abhor busy work.** Idle chitchat, paper shuffling, and clerical activity will never get you closer to meeting your goals. When top achievers are at work, they work on the tasks and activities that lead them to success. All other activities are delegated to team members who are better suited to accomplish them. Top achievers are clear about their objective and eliminate the "stuff" that gets in the way.

10. **They are exceptionally well organized.** We all operate with 24 hours in the day, yet top achievers find ways to get more done in those 24 hours. Their personal productivity is high because they keep their desks clean and their files organized, and they stay focused on their list of the six most important things they have to get done that day. Staying organized is almost like a game for them.

11. **They are great communicators.** Ronald Reagan was a master communicator and storyteller who connected with his

audience. Whether you liked his politics or not, he was able to articulate his message and make you feel good about it. By improving your communication and storytelling skills, you'll make a deeper connection with clients and prospects, which in turn leads to more business.

12. **They can motivate others.** Top achievers didn't get to the top by themselves. They realized that it takes a strong team to win. And strong teams are made up of individuals who work toward a common goal. Accordingly, top achievers help motivate others to reach their fullest potential, which in turn helps top achievers reach theirs.

13. **They practice the fundamentals.** It doesn't matter whether you're talking sports, business, or any other endeavor, you have to master the fundamentals before you achieve breakthrough success. Football is a great example; you won't win games unless you master the fundamentals of blocking and tackling. In our business, you won't reach the top unless you master the fundamentals of advice, service, and marketing. By staying focused on the basics, you can position yourself for the big breakthroughs.

14. **They are spiritual.** They have faith in God and a strong values system. Top achievers realize that we're not in this alone. They draw strength from their faith and use it as a guide in their daily living.

15. **They continually seek wisdom.** There's a story about Socrates, who had been proclaimed the wisest man in Athens by the Oracle of Delphi. Not believing what the Oracle said, Socrates started asking everyone he could find: "What is truly worthwhile in life?" He figured if somebody could answer that question, then they would certainly be wiser than he was. Everyone gave Socrates an answer, but none of the answers satisfied him; he felt those who answered were pretending to know something they really didn't know. At that point, Socrates realized he truly was

the wisest man in Athens because he knew that he didn't know it all; and because of that, he would always be searching for knowledge. Top achievers are like Socrates—they constantly seek knowledge and find new ways to move ahead.

Consistency breeds success. If you develop good habits and apply them consistently—through bull and bear markets—you'll be successful.

These 15 habits described above, combined with the nine TNT strategies, are a blueprint for achieving success in your chosen endeavor. By incorporating them into your life, you'll not only achieve greatness, but you'll enjoy the journey along the way.

SUMMARY

- There's only one difference between top achievers and average achievers—top achievers have simply cracked the code for success. By living *The 15 Habits of Top Achievers,* your life will take on a shine you never thought possible.

TNT #9 ACTION STEPS

- Study *The 15 Habits of Top Achievers.*
- Start living *The 15 Habits of Top Achievers.*

16

PUTTING IT ALL TOGETHER
How to Make It Happen—Now

"Knowing is not enough; we must apply. Willing is not enough; we must do."
—JOHANN VON GOETHE

Do you know people who always seem lucky? You know, people who get all the breaks, who have all the big accounts fall into their laps, and who don't work half as hard as you do. These are the people in the Chairman's Club, and you say, "Yeah but . . ." Ever wonder why they're so lucky? Are they just a statistical fluke, or could it be that they created their own luck? Could it be they prepared themselves to be lucky? Could it be that they positioned themselves to be the recipient of luck?

Lucky people don't exist through statistical chance. Even people who win the lottery aren't lucky. They *positioned* themselves to win by doing one simple thing—*they bought a ticket!* If you don't buy a lottery ticket, you'll never win the lottery—it's that simple. And even though buying a lottery ticket won't guarantee that you will win, it will dramatically increase your odds. It's no different with the material in this book.

If you don't implement the ideas you learned in this book, then you've wasted your time. On the other hand, if you roll up your sleeves, get focused, and start implementing, you'll be well on your way to personal and professional success.

So how do you go about implementing our plan? To help you, we've identified three critical steps.

First, review the nine TNT steps and memorize them. Create a clear picture of each step and how it fits into the overall plan. Here's a quick review for you.

The Four Foundation Steps

#1. Gain Personal and Professional Clarity through the Blueprinting Process—identify your top values, find your meaningful purpose, create a compelling vision for your future, develop a personal and professional mission statement, and set SMAC-certified goals so you have a clear road map going forward.

#2. Get the Right People on the Team—classify your staff into A+, A, B, C, or D, and within the next 90 days make sure you have only A or A+ staff members remaining so you can move forward with the best team possible.

#3. Systematize Everything—create a Systems Manual that contains a form, letter, checklist, or step-by-step procedure for every activity in your office, including back-office activities, marketing, personnel, and technology, so you can deliver a high level of service on a consistent basis.

#4. Improve Your Effectiveness—write down your six most important activities every day and stay focused on doing the most productive thing at every given moment so you can accomplish more without working more hours.

The Four RevenueGenerating Steps

#5. Build Your Brand—implement the VIPER strategy to build a brand that makes you stand out so you can attract top clients.

#6. Build Relationships and Communicate—focus on people, not products, so you can develop a meaningful relationship with them that transcends business-to-consumer marketing.

#7. Focus Marketing Efforts on Top Clients and Prospects— show them love so they'll reciprocate by working with you and sending you referrals.

#8. Deliver Client Events—provide ongoing education and entertainment so you can stay top of mind with your clients and provide a safe place for referrals to get to know you.

The Successful Habits Step

#9. Follow *The 15 Habits of Top Achievers*—live by the 15 habits that are shared by successful achievers, and you will become and remain a successful achiever too.

Second, schedule two appointments with yourself each week for the next 12 months to work on this material. Each appointment should be two hours long. Assume that the appointment you set with yourself is really with an A+ client. That means you should only break it in an emergency. Don't break it to schedule a meeting with another client; that meeting can be rescheduled. And don't fall into the trap of letting the appointment you set with yourself slide because you're too busy doing other stuff. If you let that happen, you'll never get back to implementation.

Third, celebrate small victories along the way. Each time you complete a step or an activity and you feel especially proud of it, treat yourself. Take your family out to dinner. Buy a little present for yourself or your spouse or kids. Go to a sporting event. It's very important that you recognize the progress you're making because that will give you positive reinforcement and keep you motivated to stay on track.

IT'S YOUR TIME

No matter how hard we try to help you or how simple we make this plan for you to follow, some of you reading this will fail. Some of you will read this book and think that something magical will happen; and that just by reading it, your life and your business will change forever. Unfortunately, it doesn't work that way. You're not going to get from point A to point Z without exerting some serious effort.

In the first few months of following this plan, you'll end up working more hours. These steps are time-consuming, no doubt about it. But, sometime in the next 12 months, you'll reach a crossover point where the amount of time you spend is less and the results you achieve are more. You'll reach that point when you're clear on your mission and vision, you've got A+ and A staff, you're totally systematized, and you're focused on deepening your relationship with your top clients and prospects. How long it takes to get to that point varies from advisor to advisor, but it could easily take 9 to 18 months. Just don't give up!

We began the book by talking about the three secrets to success, which are Relentless Burning Desire, Love Affair Marketing, and Systemization. But the greatest of these is Relentless Burning Desire. Find yours and follow it. Don't take the path of least resistance. Take the path near the cliff. The results you get and the exhilaration you feel will be directly proportional to how far you get out of your comfort zone.

So what are you waiting for?

"If one advances confidently in the direction of his dreams,
And endeavors to live the life which he has imagined,
He will meet with a success unexpected in common hours."
—HENRY DAVID THOREAU

Retirement plans, 73–74
Risks, 45
Rituals, xiii
Road Not Taken, The (Frost), xv
Role-playing, 96–97

S

salary.com, 71
Scheduling, 155
Schwab, Charles, 151
Schwartz, Tony, 160
Sculley, John, 35
Self-confidence, 94
Service
    good *vs.* world-class, xii
    offerings, reviewing, 223
Simmons, Annette, 207
Six degrees of separation, 229
"Six most important," 140,
    151–53, 157, 263
Sleep, 164–65
SMAC goals, 52–53. *See also*
    Goals
Smiling, 188
Socrates, 3, 265–66
SONY, 175
Southwest Airlines, xi, 37, 117
Spirituality, 265
Sposa, Mike, 119
Staff. *See also* Compensation, of
    staff; Hiring staff
    benefits, 73–74
    empowerment of, 150
    evaluating current, 75–82,
        268
    firing poor performers,
        76, 110
    interns, 86
    meetings, 147
    mismatches, 94
    new employee checklist,
        108
    personal notes in
        newsletter, 215
    systemization and, 123–24

training with
    systemization, 118
Starbucks, xii, 180
Stories, value clarification and,
    14–15
Story Factor, The (Simmons), 207
Storytelling, 206–7
Stress, 155
Success
    characteristics of top
        achievers, 262–66
    code for, 261–67
    habits of top achievers,
        269
    personal definition of,
        32–33
Systemization, xiii–xiv, 115–42,
    268
    action steps, 142
    areas for, 121
    benefits of systems,
        116–20, 141
    birthday calls and, 212
    bonus plan and, 124–25
    comprehensive example
        of, 127–30
    referral requests, 232–37
    revising as needed, 127
    sample prospect/referral
        follow-up system, 131–41
    staff and, 123–24
    system as solution, 120–27
    system defined, xiii,
        121–22
    Systems Manual, 120, 122,
        141

T

Tax shelters, 200
Team leader, 78, 79, 83–84
Templeton, John, 24
Thoreau, Henry David, 270
Time, as commodity, 44–45,
    175, 191
Time blocking, 154–55

Time management. *See*
    Effectiveness
Time Management Tracking
    Sheet, 146, 167
TNT steps
    foundation steps, 268
    revenue generating steps,
        268–69
    successful habits steps, 269
Trading systems, 121, 125,
    134–35
Transfers systems, 121, 125,
    133–34
Trust, 176

U–V

Updates system, 121, 126,
    137–38
Value, 174–76
    creating sustainable, 175
    time and, 175
    trust and, 176
    wisdom and, 175–76
Values, 12–20, 173–74
    benefits of, 13–14
    clarifying, 14–20
    of client, 203–4
    exercise, 19
    stories and, 14–15
VIPER™, 172–83, 191, 268
    experience, 180
    Grateful Dead and,
        181–83
    intimacy, 177–79
    personality, 179–80
    respect, 180–81
    vision/values/value, 172–76
Vision, 29–42, 153, 172–73,
    262–63
    advisory council and, 222
    of client, 204
    creating picture of, 33–35
    defined, 31
    describing to job
        candidates, 94

Share the message!

Bulk discounts
Discounts start at only 10 copies and range from 30% to 55% off
retail price based on quantity.

Custom publishing
Private label a cover with your organization's name and logo.
Or, tailor information to your needs with a custom pamphlet
that highlights specific chapters.

Ancillaries
Workshop outlines, videos, and other products are available on
select titles.

Dynamic speakers
Engaging authors are available to share their expertise and insight
at your event.

**Call Dearborn Trade Special Sales at
1-800-621-9621, ext. 4444,
or e-mail trade@dearborn.com**